Mummy

With my love

Sue

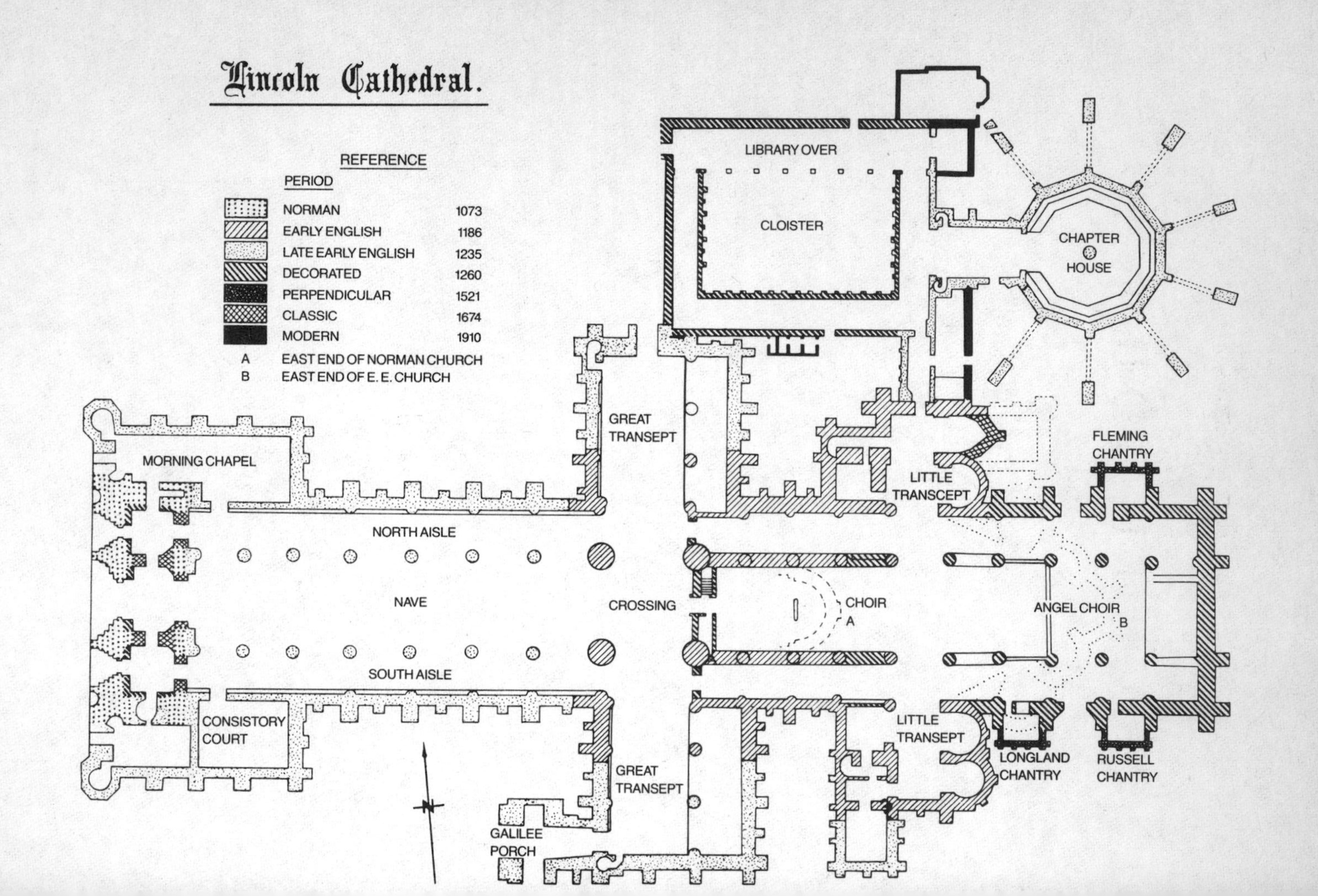
Lincoln Cathedral.
REFERENCE
PERIOD
NORMAN 1073
EARLY ENGLISH 1186
LATE EARLY ENGLISH 1235
DECORATED 1260
PERPENDICULAR 1521
CLASSIC 1674
MODERN 1910
A EAST END OF NORMAN CHURCH
B EAST END OF E. E. CHURCH
LIBRARY OVER
CLOISTER
CHAPTER HOUSE
MORNING CHAPEL
GREAT TRANSEPT
LITTLE TRANSCEPT
FLEMING CHANTRY
NORTH AISLE
NAVE
CROSSING
CHOIR
A
ANGEL CHOIR
B
SOUTH AISLE
CONSISTORY COURT
LITTLE TRANSEPT
GREAT TRANSEPT
LONGLAND CHANTRY
RUSSELL CHANTRY
GALILEE PORCH

THE CATHEDRAL

Behind open doors –
talking with people who give
their lives to a cathedral

DANNY DANZIGER

VIKING

VIKING

Published by the Penguin Group
27 Wrights Lane, London W8 5TZ, England
Viking Penguin Inc., 40 West 23rd Street, New York, New York 10010, USA
Penguin Books Australia Ltd, Ringwood, Victoria, Australia
Penguin Books Canada Ltd, 2801 John Street, Markham, Ontario, Canada, L3R 1B4
Penguin Books (NZ) Ltd, 182–190 Wairau Road, Auckland 10, New Zealand

Penguin Books Ltd, Registered Offices: Harmondsworth, Middlesex, England

First published 1989
10 9 8 7 6 5 4 3 2 1

Printed in Great Britain by
Richard Clay Ltd, Bungay, Suffolk
Filmset in 12/14 pt Garamond

A CIP catalogue record for this book is available from the British Library

ISBN 0-670-81962-X

CONTENTS

INTRODUCTION

My first sight of the Cathedral was an agonizingly protracted one. It was one of our bi-annual bicycling weekends, this time in February, and I had chosen Lincolnshire, on the basis that it was flat. The Lincolnshire Wolds, however, are not flat; they are very, very hilly. They are also very beautiful, and I yearn to visit them again, but not by bike, and not in February, when the east winds storm across the Siberian plains to whip through the tender parts of eastern England.

Forty miles, perhaps less, was the day's target, but the wind was so fierce and the hills so steep that it seemed unlikely we would reach our destination in time. We could see journey's end, Lincoln, in the awesome shape of the Cathedral, which never for a moment was obscured by a bend or a hill that entire day. And that night, having missed the train, all tiredness vanished as we walked round and round the Cathedral, all lit up in gold, gasping at the beauty of this wonderful building, further enhanced by a perfect crescent moon and a night sky, bright and clear, with more stars crammed into the heavens than we had ever seen before. Very early in the morning, a time when unfit cyclists are normally sound asleep, particularly young Wilmot and Josh, we went to communion and then, after breakfast, we went on a tour of the Cathedral, persuading a passing official, who I now know is Gordon Lauder, to take us up the Central Tower for a view that, for any of us, has still not been bettered.

That was four years ago – and I had not forgotten that magical day and night. I was back in Lincoln to write a profile of an English town. Lincoln had seemed about right, neither north nor south, neither rich nor poor, no longer primarily agricultural nor predominantly industrial. I was living in 20 Minster Yard, one of the properties owned by the Cathedral. I met the Dean and my neighbours, Katie, the verger, and her husband, Kevin, who sings in the choir. I quite rapidly got to know the Subdean and the organist; I met the Clerk of Works, and Mark Dicken, who runs the Fabric Fund. I made friends all over the place. For ten days, outside my window, which overlooked the West End, the Norman front of the Cathedral, I could see the conservator, John Hurd, renovating the great West Door with infinite care and attention. It took me a couple of weeks to realize that I was completely out of my mind – it was not the town I should be writing about, but the Cathedral, and once I had decided I immediately changed tack.

If there is one area where our past is seen to be a foreign land, our ancestors as incomprehensible as visitors from Mars, one needs look no further than the cathedrals to find that evidence. They are the most phenomenal expression of spirituality: taking sometimes centuries to complete, these buildings stretched the technology of their time to the limit, and not for any functional purpose, but for the glory of God.

We have built nothing quite like those great cathedrals in this age. We have very tall buildings, we have very big buildings, we have some very odd buildings, but never will we make another building in the same spirit as that of the masons and craftsmen who created those palaces, nor with the far-sightedness of the kings and clergymen who initiated them, knowing full well they would not live to see them completed.

But what we have done is to look after them; we have cared for them, we have repaired them, and even, occasionally, we have rebuilt them. We cherish them in our thoughts, we remember them in legacies, and by visiting them and donating money at the door, we help pay for their upkeep. We have, for the most part, been responsible guardians. There is a huge reservoir of affection for our cathedrals (every cathedral in every area of the country is 'our cathedral'). It is not just because of their awesome, unparallelled beauty, but also because they are bound up with the history and heritage of this land; they are landmarks and they are rallying places in times of adversity as well as celebration.

What I hope you will discover through these interviews is how a cathedral – in this case, a cathedral nine centuries old – is neither an architectural nor a spiritual anachronism, but a real living organism. Perched on a hill, Lincoln Cathedral dominates the city and is visible for thirty-nine miles in most directions. Built by order of William I in 1076, it is a cathedral that most of the kings and queens of England have visited, and where history has more than once been played out. It was here that Edward II created his son Prince of Wales, and, centuries later, during the Second World War, it was the place the RAF pilots aimed for when they came back to home base, exhausted or exhilarated from flying sorties. I, for one, had never given thought to the army of people who live for a cathedral. I have talked to thirty-nine people about what they do, in, on and around the Cathedral, from Ben Kendal, the 12-year-old chorister, to the retiring Dean, the Very Reverend Honourable Oliver Twisleton-Wykeham-Fiennes and to the new Dean, of course; from Cynthia Smith, the cleaner, to Mick O'Connor, the stonemason who works on the building; from Effie Mansfield, the switchboard operator, to Lyndon Matthews, the police constable whose beat includes the Cathedral. Along the way we have talked about God, and this extraordinary building, and the pride they have for what they do, for it is evident that each one of them considers his or her work to be a privilege and joy to undertake.

The time I spent in Lincoln was very precious; I wanted it never to end. Now that I'm back home, in London, I miss the people there, I miss that uniquely awful Lincolnshire weather, I even miss the bells – the bells that toll from 7 a.m. until 11 p.m.; the bell-ringing practice on Thursday evening, which seems to go on all night; the bells on Sundays, which hardly stop pealing – but most of all, I miss the Cathedral.

Facing that lovely West End all those months I was there, I could never stop marvelling at the scope and the detail of it every time I looked up from my desk. Then I would be distracted and have to walk around the entire building, where another view or detail of the Cathedral would delight and distract me once again. And there would be someone I knew, Edna Parker, the flower arranger, Juliet Montague, the Deacon, Christopher Laurence, the Archdeacon, or one of the work force: 'Haven't you finished your book yet?' The Cathedral on a hot summer's day, dark and cool and calm inside, despite hundreds of tourists milling about; the winter sun setting on the beautiful west face, picking up the warmth of the soft, honey-brown stone; that fierce wind around Minster Yard; the unexpected views of the Cathedral, suddenly, from a petrol station, a pub garden, or a lane dozens of miles away – all these things I will remember.

There are two special memories that will stay with me. The first one is this. I started to run while I was there; three times a week I would run around what was first the cricket grounds, and then, after a peculiar overlap, when there were nets and a cricket score-board, four rugby posts, and a couple of hockey goalmouths. But before I headed out to the fields, I would run around the Cathedral. On my very first run it was raining on the south side, raining quite hard – and there was blazing sunshine around Nettle Yard on the north side. I ran around again, and then once more, and still that was happening . . . well, it is a very big building.

The second special memory is of a Remembrance Day service. I believe there were 4,000 worshippers, half the number that came for Christmas carols, when there were four live camels tethered on the West Green. That Remembrance Day I was sitting at my desk, speaking on the telephone to my younger brother. I had finished all my interviews, I was telling him. And for half an hour, as we talked, I watched everyone coming out of the Cathedral: the Mayor; the editor of the *Lincolnshire Echo*; Katie, the verger, in her smartest blue cassock worn only on special occasions; the Bishop, with his prop-forward physique, smiling and joking with members of the congregation; Colin Walsh, the new organist, with his Alsatian, Daniel; John Harvey, the steward, limping slightly (he's waiting for his hip replacement operation); Mollie Bilcliffe, 88 years young; young Ben Kendal (his father is in the police force) . . . And as I described all these people to Jimmy, and I looked at all the other people there I shall never meet, I thought how much I have enjoyed writing this book, and how much I shall miss Lincoln.

DR JOHN BAILEY, CLERK OF WORKS

I DON'T think there is any parallel today. The space programme is the nearest we've got to where a nation pushes the boat out and does something for reasons that they feel are very important. If you exclude from the space race the militaristic empire-building aspect of it, and look upon it as that huge surge of emotion of man to reach for something that seems to be outside man's capacity, like to stand and walk on the moon – that moment is probably the nearest thing to the sort of experience that people went through building these places. You've got to remember that when Lincoln was being built, Beverley was being built, York was being built, Southwell was being built, Winchester was being built – all the major cathedrals were being built at the same time, and they represented the absolute limits of man's ability to create, and the people believed it is through the act of creation that man is the nearest to the Creator. So these cathedrals are the most phenomenal expressions, and there is nothing to touch them outside the medieval period.

I don't think any society would create such huge monuments without a feeling that they were expressing something very important to themselves and to their society. They built them not for any functional purpose, but for the glory of God. It was an expression of the fact that if you could get to that level of experience, it was the nearest you could actually physically get to God; and through the physical action, the spiritual release came.

They were engineers and craftsmen of the first magnitude. Certainly, as sophisticated as any that've been seen before or since, and, I suspect, probably, time for time, we haven't got their equal any more. They were virtuosi. We haven't got the actual manual skills now, and one of my problems is to find carvers who can carve like you see in the Cathedral, and can set stone in the same way. The audacity of what they did – bearing in mind they didn't have Portland cement and hydraulic mortars; they didn't even have a mortar that would set solid, so they used lime, which took maybe ten years to set. They had no mechanical hoist mechanisms, they had no steel, they had only wrought iron, so all their scaffolding and hoists were hessian-rope and wood, and manpower.

They didn't work as we do now, in as much as they didn't actually draw plans. They used geometrical measure, proportion and description, which go right back to the Greeks. If you go to one of these cathedrals and try to work it out by linear measurement, by measuring things, you are constantly mystified by the inaccuracies. You use your eyes in there and you will see huge inaccuracies, *this* bay, *this* fount, *this* piece of carving, is different to *that* bay, *that* piece of carving. But the joy of these places, the reason they vibrate, is because they have an enormous amount of variety in them. Medieval buildings represent and describe experiences, they aren't mechanical, like classical buildings, which are done on linear measurements.

There is nothing in these buildings that is not ordered if you know how to read the language, important theological, spiritual symbolisms: the cross itself, the centre of the tower being the heart. They are all part and parcel of a way of expressing abstract theological concepts in built forms, and we don't do that today at all, that's something quite dead. The idea of religious numbers or religious ideas in the fabric of the building is everywhere. You can see it as a spiritual experience solidified. Three is the favourite number because it's the Trinity, and you find it constantly being used in vaulting, in arcading, in little runs of lancet windows, threes: Father, Son, Holy Ghost; Father, Son, Holy Ghost; Father, Son, Holy Ghost.

They were stretching technology all the time to the limits and, of course, we see only what didn't fall down. Remember, lots fell down because they went too far – it was too high, too thin. What they were doing was refining, refining, refining, getting it smaller and smaller and smaller, until you get columns that defy logic that they should stay in place, walls that, from the inside particularly, defy gravity. You went in through that door at the West End, and you went into a world that was a transitional period between you and Heaven, and it was so huge and it was so light that it defied human understanding. And they would have painted those vaults like the skies of Heaven, blue with stars in, and the whole thing would have lifted you up. Going in to a place like that has a huge impact, particularly if you were a medieval peasant; you would have a physical response to it, you would drop to your knees – and they did that, there's plenty of descriptions of people going in to a church and prostrating themselves with the sheer nearness of God to them within that place. It even happens to the tourists today. If you watch people go into the place, they start to whisper, they tiptoe about. That impact is still strong.

Because they were generally built of local stone, each cathedral has its own particular characteristics. Lincoln has a colour that is fairly unique, this warm brown, nicotine-colour stone is iron and stone which gives it a curious, rich colour. English churches tend to be low and fat, a slightly dumpy, pregnant sort of look to them, whereas Lincoln is tall and thin and slender, and, of course, its siting on the edge of the escarpment means that it is set in a very dramatic location, particularly coming from the south side, where you see it up on the horizon.

My first sight of it was the view from the road coming in from the east, where you see it with three fingers pointing up, and if you see that in the dusk, it really is a stunning experience. I was visiting Gothic buildings everywhere, I wasn't just coming here. It was an accident in the first instance of coming across Lincoln amongst a lot of other cathedrals. But I think Lincoln does have a certain grip on people, that when they experience that shock of seeing it for the first time, and walk around in it, it's a sort of love affair. And once it's hit you, you don't forget it.

If you walk around the Cathedral, you don't need to be an expert to see how the chemical impurities in the atmosphere are attacking the stone. You can see the stone sort of peeling off, as though it is bursting from inside, and that is purely the attack of sulphates – and that is all over the whole Cathedral. The rate of decay and attack by pollutants is such that we are actually running as fast as we can but still going backwards.

There is nothing dramatic happening, like the tower falling down or the West Front falling off; what you've got here is a multiplicity of minor crises. Each one in itself is no big deal, but multiply these by the hundred and you start to get an understanding of the problem. On the stone side we've got this perpetual chemical attack on the physical face of the stone. Lead that covers the roofs is a marvellous material, but after sixty years, or something like that, it starts to get fatigue, just like metal fatigue in aircraft; it's expanding and contracting with the heat and cold, and in the end it cracks. That means water gets through and rots the timber underneath, so you've got to strip the lead off to repair the timber, which has been rotted by water or attacked by beetles, and then put it all back again. Fortunately, we can reuse lead, so it is an extremely efficient material; in fact, we are doing the south transept right this minute. One side is done, but it's like painting the Forth Bridge: you go round the Cathedral once every seventy-five, eighty years, and then you're back to square one and you start again.

My predecessors have been sitting here since 1150, looking after this Cathedral in its various shapes and sizes, and there is no reason why it can't go on. There's a feeling that if those people could keep this place going, surely to God you can. In fact, it's a support, because otherwise a place like this would be so daunting that you would just give up. But the fact is that there have been people here for centuries, rebuilding it, repairing it, caring for it and using it, and you look around and you say, 'Well, they were presumably ordinary people, no doubt I can look after it as well.' One feels a kinship, a rapport with one's predecessors. I've known several who have been here. Dear old Fred Higgins was here when I first came; he has just been buried in the Cathedral and I'm cutting his burial stone at the moment. You get a very strong feeling of continuity in a place like this.

I don't think you would do this sort of job if you didn't have some kind of love affair with the building – you don't get people working here for the money. On a summer's evening, at eight o'clock, if you just go in to the Cathedral all by yourself, nobody else there, it's absolutely quiet and there is that almost green evening light coming into it, all the strain and stress just drifts away. It's the most astonishing thing.

I am, in fact, a Quaker, and Quakers don't believe in the need for cathedrals or churches of any sort, or for clergy for that matter. I think I'm unique in that sense. And I think I'm the only Quaker ever to have his own stall in the choir of the Cathedral. *Clericus Fabricus*, it says, and that's me.

I think it's sad that society today hasn't got the equivalent to this. Of course, to say we should be building great cathedrals is pie-in-the-sky, because you can't put the clock back. But I think it's symptomatic of illness in a society if it doesn't have some thrust of this sort of magnitude. We do occasionally express it in commercial buildings, things like the Pompidou Centre in Paris or the new Exchange Building in London, or some of the major buildings in America. Things like the space programme have an element of this desire to actually push the boat out, as I said, but the world is in a trough at the moment where it doesn't have an equivalent urge to express this need to push out the boundaries until you fall off the edge. We've explored the world and there's nothing much left to go and see: we've climbed all the mountains and we've gone down to the bottom of the oceans. It's all rather small scale, rather materialistic and rather ephemeral, most of the stuff we do. It may well be that our concerns are for a material future, while their concerns were for a spiritual future.

THE REVEREND DEDRA BELL, DEACONESS

I GREW up in the Anglican Church in Miami, Florida. My mother was a Methodist, my father was Anglican, and when they married my mother converted to the Anglican Church.

I was at a conference of North American deans, and Dean Fiennes was there as a visitor. We met and he said the Dean and Chapter of Lincoln were looking for a woman priest to join them for six months – would I be interested? So we sat and we talked, and, yes, I was very interested. I had never been to Great Britain before, had never really had the chance to see firsthand my roots as an Anglican, and so for me it was going to be a wonderful opportunity. The only restriction that was placed on me was that it had to be very clear, and I had to understand and agree, that when I came here I would not be able to function publicly as a priest, that the sacramental roles were not allowed. I was willing to agree to that for a trial period of six months.

I took the 18.04, which is the non-stop train from King's Cross. It was late August, so it was getting dark earlier, and as we approached Lincoln there was this massive structure all lit up and darkness all round it. It was very frightening, but also very exciting, just the thought of being in a place that had history that goes back before the existence of the United States. I was met at the train by the Dean, who said, 'Did you see the little building?' 'Yes, I did!'

After you spend a bit of time here, you don't really have a sense that it's old, because there's still life and there's still activity, and people milling around, working to keep this place for at least another 900 years.

I arrived on a Thursday, and the first time they really saw me was that Sunday in church, although they had been told of my imminent arrival. Mollie Bilcliffe, who is a wonderful woman who lives right around the corner, said that it took her a while to get used to me because I was 'pretty and had all this red hair'. She said, 'Once I realized you really were a minister and a priest, it made all the difference,' but she said it took her about four months.

I have never had a problem with men as far as separating my priestly ministry from my social life, and didn't find that I had that problem here either. I have my own rules, and my most basic rule is that I never date any men from the parish where I live. People always have this impression that clergy are asexual, have no kind of sex life whatsoever, and that's not true. In fact, for me, my sexuality and my spirituality are very much intertwined, although at the moment I don't have a sex life.

The relationship that I have with other people is in many ways how I am strengthened and encouraged and informed in my relationship with God, and it has to be very clear, and understood, that I am a sexual person, whether I participate in sexual activities or not. I am a person who has needs and desires, and wants, and ambitions and hopes and prayers. That all takes me back to my relationship with God, who is the one I go to when I want to work out some of my needs and desires, my wants and prayers, and frustrations.

Probably part of the reason that I am still single at 31 is because it is very hard for men in this day and age to understand how I could make such a commitment in my choice of career and still be willing to be a woman and feminine. My husband is going to have to be particularly understanding of things like me going to work at five o'clock on Sunday mornings, which I have a habit of doing. I don't necessarily want him to be a priest – I think one in the house is more than enough – but I think that it might be healthy if he were at least a Christian.

For me, I think that the reason I have been called to this peculiar ministry of the priesthood is a need and a want to share in the sacramental life of the body of Christ – it's not just for the clergy, it's not just for lay people, but all of us together, continually learning about this faith that we have, and how we act that out in our lives.

I never functioned publicly as a priest in Lincoln as agreed. That was a very hard thing to do, to realize that when I went to church on Sundays, I never could preside over the Eucharist. I got to the point where I had a need to function as a sacramental minister, and that became very draining on me. If they had approved of ordained women, I would have stayed on.

It took me a long time to adjust back to life back in the States, and I often think about the people I met in Lincoln.

MOLLIE BILCLIFFE, FLOWER ARRANGER

MY mother was one of ten and my father was one of ten, and they were both very good church people and automatically we went to church every Sunday, wearing all our Sunday clothes. I have always been very, very attached to my church.

I left school in 1918, and I nursed until I was married. My husband was a house surgeon at the county hospital. When he arrived at Lincoln station for his appointment on a very foggy and cold night, he thought that it would be for just six months, and in fact he spent the rest of his life in Lincoln.

I came up to see him several times – we were engaged at that point – and I stayed at the White Hart. We were very much in love and we were married shortly afterwards.

The first time I came here it was a very cold November night, and we arrived about half-past seven. It was very dark – of course, the Cathedral wasn't lit in those days – but I saw this enormous building and even in moonlight it was magnificent. I was terribly impressed.

On the Sunday I went to the first service I had been to, and that was lovely. My husband was a High Churchman and he went to St Swithin's Church downhill, but I always went to the Cathedral, and when he realized that I wasn't going anywhere else, he decided to come with me.

The dean then was Dean Fry. I've known five deans and seven bishops. Dean Fry was a difficult old man, not a very friendly person. He had a little square beard, I remember, although all the Chapter had beards in those days, except the precentor, who was clean-shaven.

The extraordinary thing is that we always used to call the bishops 'my lord', and then as the bishops came and went, they were Simon and Kenneth, and . . . Bob! I don't think we were perhaps as friendly in the old days with them as we are now. It's a different sort of atmosphere now somehow.

I had four babies very quickly. The war was some years after we got here. I was still very involved with my family for the war years and I didn't do anything in the Cathedral at all. I had a tremendous number of evacuees from London billeted on me – we had as many as twenty people in the house.

All the glass in the Rose Window was taken out and buried for safety. People were guarding the building – they were on duty looking out after the fire bombs had fallen, that sort of thing. There were two or three quite nasty incidents: the hospital was hit, and one of the aircraft coming back from Germany fell on the schoolhouse, and there were a tremendous number of casualties and all the crew were killed.

I'm now 88 and, having worked as treasurer in the Cathedral for many, many years, I retired, but I do flowers for weddings and any extra sort of occasion if they need me, and I hope I shall be able to do that for a bit. I love doing the flowers, I absolutely love it. I've always been mad about flowers and gardening, and it's an enormous pleasure and a great privilege to be able to do them here.

In the early days we had just the odd visitor. I suppose because there weren't so many cars people didn't come. But now, of course, it's quite extraordinary: crowds of people come. I have long conversations with them. When you do flowers in the Cathedral, everybody comes up and talks to you: 'Do you do these every day?' And then they ask you about the flowers. In fact, it's a bit difficult sometimes because you can't get on, they ask you so many questions. I love meeting them all, although some of them ask very stupid questions.

But they're all so interested and impressed, and they all say this is the most wonderful cathedral. I don't know whether they really mean that, but they all say it. I met some very interesting people from New Zealand this morning, they were absolutely enchanted with it.

I never go away at Easter because I love it in the Cathedral, it's quite beautiful. It's a great celebration. The music and the flowers are magnificent and the singing is so beautiful – somehow there's something extra special about Easter. The congregation in the Cathedral usually each give a pound towards a lily, and so we are able to have lilies everywhere, with other flowers, of course, because lilies are expensive. The flowers at Easter are quite beautiful, and it's all very inspiring.

My age is now such that I don't really think much about the future. Not much good my making plans, is it really? I've a very happy, exciting life because there's something happening all the time and one knows so many charming and delightful people. It's a lovely atmosphere around the Cathedral, everybody's very kind and hospitable, and if you're ill, goodness me, everybody will help you.

I'm very fortunate because I don't have a great deal to worry about. I lead a very simple life. I don't smoke and I don't drink – because I don't like it, not because of any principle – and I suppose really there are no problems. I've had a miserable time with my hip replacements and that sort of thing, but I'm able to get around and I've got a splendid family, they're marvellous, and they look after me. I live alone, but I like it.

I expect my ashes will be in the cloister, but I haven't really thought about that. I hope I have a nice funeral. I have made plans about that: lots of Easter hymns, lots of flowers, and lots of good music and no dirge! I have been to a good many funerals in the Cathedral where that terrible dirge goes on at the organ – enough to kill anybody. Death, it's so depressing.

I've been, of course, to so many weddings. I can remember Bishop Greaves's daughter being married, I can't remember how long ago, but there was the most awful gale and she had to be carried from the precentory to the Cathedral. Nobody could stand up.

In the winter it's absolutely freezing. We have heating on at Christmas, and it has to go on about a month beforehand. After Christmas, it's turned off, and it is very, very cold indeed. Most of the inhabitants realize this and so we go about with four jerseys on and carry hot-water bottles.

Sermons were very long when we were first here, they went on and on. They do a bit now, actually. I think ten minutes is enough for any sermon. I suppose it's difficult for them to get all they want to say in, but on a very cold morning when you sit for twenty-five minutes, you are very cold and it's a bit boring. I'm very deaf and I wear a hearing aid, and I'm afraid I often switch off.

I get teased about my love for this place. I've just been staying with my daughter and son-in-law, and when we sat down for breakfast the other morning, I asked if there was any news, and my son-in-law said, 'Yes, just this one thing, the Cathedral's fallen down.' They pull my leg about the Cathedral because they know it's my life, although I don't do nearly as much as I used to do. This morning I went into the Cathedral to do the flowers. One of the helpers, it was her birthday, and so we all went into the coffee shop and had coffee and cakes, and we had a real party, which was great fun.

JUDITH BLOOMFIELD, BELL-RINGER

BOTH my parents are bell-ringers, and they've been ringing since they were about 16 – years and years. They sort of met through ringing. I've got two older brothers and neither of them was in the least bit interested, and consequently both of my parents were determined to get one of the three children ringing.

When we come home after practice or ringing on a Sunday, quite often we discuss the standard of ringing and if anybody made any mistakes, and why.

Probably the best thing about ringing is meeting new people because wherever you go in the country there's bound to be a tower within a mile or two of where you're staying, and anywhere there are bells, there'll be bell-ringers. You just go along to the local practice and say, 'Hi, I'm a ringer . . . can I ring?' And they welcome you in, and you go to the pub afterwards, so it's a good way of meeting people and making friends.

When I first went to Manchester, I joined the University Guild of Change Ringers. We've got our own tower, which we ring at regularly on a Sunday. There's about twenty-five of us, and we go to the pub afterwards, and go for walks on a Sunday. We're going on holiday together, a camping holiday down to the Welsh Borders. We're going to visit a lot of towers in the area, walking everywhere, and having a good social life the rest of the time.

I tend not to tell people about my bell-ringing because most people don't understand; they think bell-ringing just consists of standing in a cold church with a piece of bell-rope, sort of pulling it about a bit, so it's easier to keep quiet and not say anything very much.

People also think that most bell-ringers are quite ancient – and a lot of them are! But to keep the thing going, you've got to have new people starting all the time, and it's far easier to teach people when they're in their teens than it is when they're getting older, because in older people the brain slows down, and they also find it physically not so easy. Old people can't lift their arms up above their heads straight; even my mother comments her arms no longer go straight.

I see bell-ringing as a hobby, but some of the older ringers devote their life to ringing. They'll go 200 miles to attempt a peal; they're willing to do anything for ringing. For me it's a way of meeting other people, but at the same time I enjoy ringing – it's stimulating, you've got to think hard, get your brain working.

You could say that the majority of bell-ringers, particularly at cathedrals, tend to be fairly intellectual, because there's quite a high standard of intelligence required to ring complicated methods on twelve bells, whereas in villages, where there are only six bells, you don't have to ring such complicated methods.

ROGER BRYAN, ASSISTANT ORGANIST

I WAS one of these awful kids who instead of wanting to be an engine driver when he grew up, wanted to be a cathedral organist. I never grew out of it. So I did all the right things: went to Cambridge, got an organ scholarship there, and then came back home to Manchester to do a further post-grad course of study. This post was advertised at just the right moment – when I was finishing my post-grad study, the one piece of luck I've ever had in my life.

It's such a closed shop – I mean, it's not exactly an expanding market – that if you decide that cathedral work is what you want to do, you really have to go where the jobs are. I can't pretend that from the nappy I had a burning desire to come to Lincoln in particular, but I was lucky in the sense that I got on the second rung of the ladder in one jump. One might have expected to get assistant organist at a minor cathedral, and then perhaps go on to a more important cathedral like this.

Having tried to get a cathedral organ post for some time, I had the ridiculous situation that the same night I came back to Manchester, having been offered this post, I found out that I'd been short-listed for the assistantship at York, and the organist at Manchester Cathedral phoned the very next day asking if I was interested in *that* job.

I remember coming to Lincoln for my interview, and staying with the then-organist, Dr Marshall. I talked late into the night with him, but not about cathedrals or music; having established that we both shared the same passion for Bach, Howells and Brahms, we were talking about pre-nationalization Great Western steam railways. Philip Marshall has an enormous knowledge of, and interest in, railways, to the extent of practically having built his own working steam engine: railways and cathedrals seem somehow to go together.

I also remember him asking me if I was prepared to do a little bit of plainchant accompaniment, which rather worried me, and I remember going to bed at three o'clock feeling pretty desperate, reading through a book of plainchant accompaniment, going to sleep about five o'clock in the morning, and then waking up, absolutely shaking upright, at seven o'clock as Big Tom went off. I really didn't get very much sleep that night, but the long and short of it was my face seemed to fit, and here I still am thirteen years later, far longer than I intended to be here.

It was not a good start. I went into digs with the Archdeacon's family, which was meant to be for a few weeks, and I was still there a year later, getting increasingly uncomfortable about it and wondering when accommodation would eventually be provided. It was a difficult situation, much as I loved being with the Dudman family. Caroline and I were thinking about the future, wanting to get married, and there was the additional problem of going over to Manchester every week to do two days' teaching, while I was trying to build up teaching work here. I would get more money from two days' work there than I got in a month in the Cathedral, so it was obviously worthwhile. I used to go on the train. It was an enormously long run; you would feel pretty suicidal before you ever got there, because inevitably there was no buffet car and the heating never worked, and it went through all the places you never wanted to see, like Gainsborough, Retford, Worksop and Sheffield.

That situation lasted only for my first year, because Caroline came up to Lincoln and got a flat here, and we got engaged and decided we were going to get married the following May.

My job is to be involved and assist in all aspects of the Cathedral music, in co-operation with the organist, and to take responsibility, in his absence, for the running of the choir. Uniquely, by force of circumstances, I've worked with three colleagues, three very highly qualified, experienced and skilled cathedral musicians of very differing backgrounds and attitudes, and I think I've learned quite a lot from each of them.

When you consider that prior to Philip Marshall there'd been only four organists since the eighteenth century, it gives you some sort of perspective. I met, in his retirement, Philip Marshall's predecessor, Dr Gordon Slater, who was here from 1930 to 1966. His predecessor, Dr George Bennett, was appointed in 1895. You have to go back only two before him, that's Matthew Young, who was appointed in 1850, and his predecessor, and that takes you back to 1795. There's obviously something about the Lincoln air that breathes longevity into cathedral organists.

Philip Marshall was a very gifted musician and composer, whose particular strength lay in accompanying and improvising. I think what little abilities I may have in those directions are primarily due to his influence.

David Flood was here for only two years before being offered the post of organist at Canterbury. His legacy was to branch out in new directions and expand in different ways beyond the daily service in terms of new repertoire and new initiatives for the choir.

Colin Walsh is a first-rate musician. Colin sees his main role as consolidating what's been achieved, and making sure that we don't lose track of the day-to-day standards in performance. I think he regards the standard of excellence in the daily services as being by far the most important priority.

We have one of the finest Romantic cathedral instruments in the country, and I know that Colin is still intoxicated with it. He comes from St Albans, where they have a fairly new instrument, comparatively speaking, which was very much influenced by the neo-classical traditions, very clean and pure, but perhaps rather brittle, so the sumptuous romantic sound this instrument makes is something that he really enjoys.

It's always been a matter of policy here, not just in music, but in all spheres, that inside appointments are not made. They always – and I think the Dean is quite right – seek new blood from outside. Clearly, I've got a fairly intimate idea of the running of the music department, and of its potential and the way it could develop, but it's like assistant bank managers or deputy headmasters – you need to go elsewhere for the No. 1 appointment, and so I didn't apply when David left.

I don't suppose there's a No. 2 in the country who doesn't think that he could do the job at least as well as No. 1. That's with no disrespect to any personalities here. If I am going to stay in the world of cathedral music, I should be moving on to a No. 1 post. I hadn't intended to stay as long as I have done, but openings are few and far between, and I think it's fair to say that Lincoln is a little bit isolated and it has not always had the reputation, musically, that its stature might have indicated. I haven't got the connections that some musicians have: for example, I didn't train in London, I wasn't at one of the biggest Cambridge colleges, and, perhaps because Lincoln is a little bit isolated geographically and culturally, I don't have great opportunities for regular contact with some of the biggest cathedrals.

Also, I'm probably not sufficiently single-minded in the sense that there are other priorities in my life. I'm a family man, and I have responsibilities to my wife and my children. They see precious little of me as it is. I'm doing a job here that is nearly full-time, but, in fact, pays only a minority of my salary. I make up my income from teaching. I have to hold down four days a week schoolteaching, in my spare time as it were, to make up my income. I do quite a lot of private teaching at school, at home and in the Cathedral.

It is a frustration when you spend the majority of your time doing things you'd rather not do, because they are your bread and butter. I teach Common Entrance maths, a little bit of junior French and English as well as class music, and I teach piano at the choir school. These are not my prime interests. If I have to teach at all, I'd rather be teaching at a specialist level in diploma work, but I've got to be realistic: these are the opportunities that are offered here. I've seen too many professional musicians on the breadline because they've been standoff-ish about what they're prepared to do.

I remember, a year or two ago, giving a recital at an organists' congress and realizing that of all the other organ recitalists, there wasn't one other family person; they all were either single, separated or divorced, and I'm not prepared to carry my career ambitions to the point at which family priorities cease to be priorities. I've no doubt that if I got my publicity agent on to selling myself, I could do much more in the way of recitals. But it would be a much more insecure existence, and I'm perhaps too much of a coward to go totally freelance – and I think that I have responsibilities, as a family man, not to do that.

If I were prepared to be absolutely uncompromising, give up all my teaching at the choir school and go away and do recital work, and see even less of the family than I do at the moment, no doubt I could get my name better known at national level. I'm not prepared to go to that extent.

I have been interviewed for several No. 1 appointments – recently for the organist's post at Southwell Minster, where I was short-listed, but they appointed another candidate. It would be silly to pretend I wasn't disappointed, and a little surprised, because I felt, almost more than any other job I'd looked at, that that one might have had my name on it. And obviously, being the next cathedral down the road, I've had a lot of contact with the place and its people. I knew quite a lot about the job and felt that I could have done it as well as anyone. I think they were looking for a slightly more broadly based and kaleidoscopic musician than perhaps the conventional cathedral organist. At the end of the day – and I'm not making excuses – irrespective of experience and personality, all cathedrals are looking for very individual things, and if your face fits, all well and good.

It's not until you're short-listed for a job that you begin to assess objectively what you've got going for you. You have really caught me at a bit of a watershed. I regarded that particular post as representing a little bit of a junction. Where do we go from here? I have various options: I could say, OK, there's no prospect of an early move, so perhaps I need to think about other directions. I could think about music producing; I could perhaps go into a public school; perhaps try to find a music college lectureship. Or I could say Cheshire's my home part of the world, I'm going to go back there and have a look. My inclination at the moment is to say I'm going to stay here. I've got a good niche here. I have a good reputation and I think the Chapter have indicated, and certainly Colin Walsh is very sympathetic, they might review my job brief, which might give me a little bit more opportunity for doing things.

I never expected to be here after thirteen years. There's a danger that the longer you are in a place, and the older you get, you reach a stage where it almost begins to go against you in terms of promotion elsewhere. I suppose I came here looking at a five- to six-year apprenticeship, but cathedrals are just not like that. There are so few openings, you've got to wait for them to come up, plus you're going to have 100 or 200 competitors, so, objectively, the chances are very slim. But I am sure the right move will come up for me.

MICK CLUITT, JOINER

WHEN I first left school I worked in a one-man firm. I served my apprenticeship, then I went to a joinery manufacturer. It's only the past two years I came here. Now I'm just on the move again.

The money here's not very good, although you can just struggle by on it. Really, I just want to be my own boss; you know, come and go as you please and then it's up to me if the money comes in, isn't it?

I'm sad to leave. It's a good job and I like it, and if the money was better, I'd stop. I'm going to have to work a lot harder, more hours I mean. It won't finish at five o'clock like it does here. I'll have to go out at nights estimating for jobs and things like that. For the first year I've got a job subcontracting with a firm, and in that time I'm hoping to pull in more jobs to gradually wean off the subcontracting and go on me own. If the money's there, I'll work for it.

I want to give my kids a bit more than what they're getting now, to give them a good education if I can, look after them well, feed them, pay a few of the bills off.

That's the main reason for leaving here, but also to say that I've worked for myself, even if I don't make anything of it – just to say that I've done it. I'm coming up for 31 and I want to give it a go now; otherwise, when I retire, I'll say, 'Oh, I wish I'd done it' and it will be too late then.

I was born in Lincoln, but I never really took much notice of the Cathedral, to tell you the truth. I had the odd walk round once or twice when I was little. I've actually grown fond of it; you appreciate it more working here. When you're working here you find out things that you didn't know existed. It's nice to have a look in the roof, I'd never seen that; well, the general public don't normally see that, do they? That's interesting, that.

All the stonework, that's nice too. I'd really like to be able to go back in time and see how it was actually put up; you know, seen it worked on then, seen how it was done. That'd be good, that.

If somebody had told me I'd be interested in something like the Cathedral, I wouldn't have believed them. I'm just a normal person: go out to work, come home and sit and watch the telly. Working here hasn't changed me that much really, although it's stopped me swearing so much. And we've just come back from a holiday in Devon, and I had to have a look round Exeter Cathedral to see if it's the same as this. If I hadn't worked here, I wouldn't have bothered. Exeter I thought was very nice, but it looks like it's been only half done, half finished, because the towers just stop above the roof, they don't carry on up like ours do.

I'm going to miss this place, I must admit; the atmosphere, working with the blokes – they're a good bunch of lads and we all get on and have a good laugh. And the old people as well, because they're interesting. Some of them tell you a few stories. There's an old girl, Mrs Mac, used to live down Greestone Terrace there. She's 90, she's gone into one of these old people's homes now, but she could have told you a story or two. They're the people you want to talk to, the old people who've lived here all their lives. There's another one down Greestone, Mary Dudding, and there's Mrs Peck in Minster Yard . . . she's lived here a few years, she's a nice old biddy.

I'd like to think I'll come back to the Cathedral, but then again I'd like to think that I won't, if you see what I mean, because I want to make a go of what I'm about to do.

I can see the Cathedral's central tower and roof from my kitchen window. I wonder if I'll be wishing I was still here when I look at it . . . I don't know.

The wife's started writing one of these romance tales. Well, she reads enough of them. She sat down last night, and the night before, and she wrote two sides of a sheet of paper. I don't know if it will come to anything – have to see. Could be competition for you! The only thing I read is the paper, and I can't write very well – I'm not into writing – but I think I will read your book, with it being about the Cathedral. Yes, I'd like to sit down and read it; it could be interesting.

IAN COGHILL, CHAPTER CLERK

I CAME to Lincoln in 1977 as manager of the local Nat West Bank just around the corner, known as the Lincoln Cathedral Branch. A lot of the Cathedral business was with my branch, so I got involved with the people running the Cathedral right away, and I got to know quite a lot about the Cathedral from the business point of view.

Early in 1987, when I was 57, with three years to go until my normal retirement, I knew that at that age and stage in my career I wouldn't get offered a promotion within the bank: I would either be offered a sideways move, which I wasn't particularly keen to have, or I might be offered early retirement, which I also didn't want, as I felt I had more to offer. I knew that the bank had this scheme to second senior staff to charities – there are probably 100 senior people at any one time seconded by Nat West to major charities – and I'd heard that the present Chapter Clerk was anxious to take early retirement. Through discussions with the Dean and Chapter, I said if they felt that I could be helpful, at no cost to them – because I still would have my bank salary until my normal bank retiring age, so in effect the bank would be giving them my salary – did they think that I could be useful to them?

Correspondence started between the Dean and the bank's head office and I had interviews and so on, until in the summer of 1987 I started here. When I have been here three years from that date, I shall take my normal retirement, and they will have to replace me with somebody else, and have to pay somebody.

A Chapter Clerk is the administrative officer of the Cathedral.

I can relate it to a limited company with a board of directors: we have the five residentiary canons, who live in the close and work in the Cathedral, and they have to have a statutory meeting once a month by ecclesiastical law, like a board meeting of a company of directors.

The meeting of the Dean and Chapter is a very formal affair, and everyone addresses each other by their correct title. It is Mr Dean, Mr Subdean, Mr Chancellor, Mr Chapter Clerk, etc.; there is no Ian and Joe and Jack, none of this sort of business. I don't have any vote, of course, but I get asked for opinions on various matters, particularly if they are related to financial affairs and administration.

Each member of the Chapter has a specific job to do. The Dean is the chairman, as he is the senior canon and the second citizen of the city (after the Mayor). He is in control like a chairman of the board would be. The next senior canon is the Precentor, who is responsible for the music and for the liturgy. Then you have the Chancellor, who is responsible for the vast libraries of books and manuscripts here at Lincoln. Then we have the Subdean, who comes next in seniority and is the treasurer. He and I work closely together on the financial side. Finally, you have the Archdeacon, who is responsible to the diocese of Lincoln, so he spends part of his time here and part out in the diocese.

Like any normal meeting, we start off with apologies, cover matters arising from the previous meeting, and then we start. All sorts of things come up at meetings, administrative, financial, ecclesiastical. This next meeting we shall be discussing whether we should introduce Rite A communion service. We use Rite B at the moment, but Rite A is rather more modern. Vacant properties invariably comes up. There is a ring of properties around the Cathedral that is owned by the Dean and Chapter, which we let and have the income from to use freely as we wish. They are all mostly Grade 2 listed buildings, which need a lot of money spending on them and which become vacant from time to time. We have a long list of people who apply to rent the properties, and that often takes quite a time – who we are going to put into certain properties and so on.

The Bishop's garden party is coming up, and the Bishop has requested that we make space for sixty cars to be parked on one of our grass areas. I don't know whether they will give permission for that – I wouldn't – but little things like that take two minutes to decide.

The Church Commissioners, as the governing body of the whole of the Church of England, has property and investments all over the world. It is a huge, wealthy organization, and its vast reserves of income and property are shared throughout the Church. But the Church has to rely on that income to pay all its clergy, all its helpers and the upkeep of its churches and cathedrals. The clergy here, for instance, are not paid by the Cathedral at all; their stipends come from the Church Commissioners. Each cathedral and some churches have a percentage of the income from those properties. We don't know what that percentage is. All we know is that once a year we get a letter saying that our share of the property pool is X number of pounds for this year.

Everyone in the Dean and Chapter is pretty well clued-up. There are instances when they need advice from specialists, but you really do have to have your feet on the ground, because there are so many problems that are not religious or spiritually orientated. Things just don't happen without working for them and working at them; they will not happen just by having religious conviction. At the end of the day the Lord helps those who help themselves, and while we are living in this world, we have got to pitch our income against our expenditure.

THE REVEREND REX DAVIS, SUBDEAN

I WAS brought up in Australia and had a pretty normal kind of upbringing. My family wasn't terribly religious – I think they got rid of me on Sundays by sending me off to Sunday school. I went to a Roman Catholic school and I listened to all their doctrine and teaching with interest, although I was Church of England. I had vague premonitions of God in terms of the general consensus in which one moved, but nothing tremendously exciting.

Then my cousin, with whom I had a lot to do, was going off to confirmation classes, and I latched on to that, I suppose more for companionship and friendship than anything else. I enjoyed that and I began to become more consciously religious, although in a very uncommitted way, a very light touch to it all.

And then I had an experience that was almost one of these conversion experiences, I suppose, one of these awakenings or bursts of light, in which I suddenly found I was convinced I wanted to become ordained. I didn't know what was involved in that, I didn't know what it meant, but it suddenly became an obsession. I went along to the local church person and said that I wanted to be ordained – I think he thought it was one of the greater jokes of the week. But I persisted in this obsession and it began to clarify.

I went to university with the conviction that I wanted to study to be ordained. I joined the Evangelical Society at the University of Sydney and began to learn a lot more about Bible religion. I then went through another experience that I remember quite vividly. There has been a succession of little touches of insight or awakening right through my life. That life got put on a railroad track, which inexorably led to ordination, and since then to having a ministry in the Church of England, which has gone through many ups and downs, and changes and chances, a great deal of ecumenical experience, a great deal of re-awakening in the charismatic movement, a great deal of re-awakening with Roman Catholic friends and Pentecostal friends, all fortified by innumerable little experiences. So changes happening all the time, and changes occurring that are not premeditated, they just happen by force of circumstance or by following a particular trail.

My first sight of Lincoln was a desperately dismal experience. I had just come back from a conference in the South Pacific, and this invitation had come from the Bishop of Lincoln formally asking me if I would consider coming to Lincoln. My wife and I came up to be interviewed. We drove up the A1 and, being novices, we turned off at Newark and drove up into that long ribbon development, through North Hykeham and on and on. If you approach Lincoln from that direction, it is a pretty dreary experience of nineteenth-century housing and the industrial world.

In the far distance the Cathedral was sitting up there, but to approach the Cathedral from down below is to fight your way through Lincoln city into a wilderness of one-way streets, which became more and more depressing. At last we found a place to park, and we went to the Chancellor's house, where we were staying that night. I remember my wife was almost . . . well, she was in tears, so depressed was the whole situation.

The Cathedral seemed to represent all the things that I had been most opposed to for a long time. One speaks metaphorically, of course, but this building sends out all kinds of signals; it is a very ambiguous building. Some of the signals that it sends out are oppressive. It was a fortress cathedral, it was oppressive to the British people living here in Norman times, so for 200 years it must have been a symbol of oppression. It was a hostile kind of place, physically hostile in some ways. It represented, I think, a church captured in its history. It represented the kind of impossibility of altering or changing that kind of church, and I had been talking for years about change and renewal. I think some of that still emanates from it. At a later time it was a Gothic building, which I think represented in the twelfth and thirteenth centuries a sense of Western civilization coming of age, emerging from the cocoon of the Dark Ages and celebrating itself in a way that has never been equalled in any form of architecture. So the building is also sending out this soaring expression of human activity, of human achievement and human delight. This is its ambiguity, both celebrating human aspirations and, at the same time, being a building of domination.

You can get the ambiguity in the intractability of the place: that things will not alter or will not change. You think that you can change them, but you push and press, and, like an amoeba, it just comes back into shape again. In the worship pattern, for example, even if one changes little bits and fiddles on the fringes of it, none the less it seems extraordinarily fixed and intractable. Yet there are moments of sheer brilliance, when you see through to something much better and much greater. I have been seduced by it totally, I now see it as an Easter palace.

The Cathedral has a huge power of its own, it's got an inertia more or less, which is both comforting and profoundly disturbing. It all depends upon one's own mood of the moment as to which is reinforced. It can make you sometimes very, very angry, and it can make you sometimes almost feel a foretaste of Heaven.

But the work we do doesn't need the building. If an earthquake came and it fell down tomorrow, we would make the rubble look tidy and carry on being the Dean and Chapter of Lincoln, and doing our business. Lincoln, though, would be at a loss, because Lincoln without the Cathedral is a very dull little provincial town, and unless people came to look at the ruins, it would lose its touristic attraction.

The Dean and Chapter are the clergy responsible for the Cathedral, and church affairs are always political. There are political pressures one way or another all the time, usually with a financial base – all politics seem to be related to exchequer problems. There are all kinds of manoeuvrings going on, which one enjoys and belongs to and is fascinated by.

With the politics of contemporary partisan politics – the great left and right divide – I should suppose that the Dean and Chapter are roughly divided as most of the nation is divided; let's put it two-fifths right wing and three-fifths vaguely left wing, but not getting their act together.

Once you begin to talk of politics with a big 'P', once you begin to be aware of Third World problems, the South Africa question, the issue of nuclear weapons, ecology and the greenhouse effect, etc., etc., there is no way in which you can perceive these issues and not be political.

Whether or not money is put into *this* project rather than *that* project, whether you think that non-stipendiary ministry is the great thing of the future or traditional ministry is the great thing to be preserved, whether you believe in the ordination of women or not – that's politics with a small 'p', and you use all your skills as a manipulator of people to move one way or the other.

Once you begin to take God seriously, you have to be political. God is the great politician in the sense that he has given us the challenge of trying to discover what redemption means in our own world. And to do that is to really put us in the forefront of being political. It is a great gamble what God did in the incarnation, and a great gamble in what is going on with humankind. So if you take God seriously, you have got to be involved politically.

MARK DICKEN, FABRIC FUND

MY father was vicar of a country parish in Nottinghamshire. By climbing to the top of the horse-chestnut tree in the garden on a clear day I could see Lincoln Cathedral, although it was equally visible on a clear day from the top of the church tower in the village.

Living in Nottinghamshire in the early to mid-Fifties was a time of relative economic depression, when we were only just coming out of austerity and there was a shortage of all sorts of commodities. My mother periodically would go to Lincoln, because that was the county town, if she wanted to go shopping for special things, like material to make new curtains or something of that sort. I, as one of three children, was dragged along on these outings whether I liked it or not.

I remember climbing the hill to the Cathedral on an occasion when the organ was being overhauled, and there were all the guts of the organ laid out on the floor in the north transept. I still have a vision in my mind's eye of that, and I have to say that in a curious way the Cathedral stirred me.

I wouldn't want to give you the impression that my happiness at being here is totally unequivocal – it isn't. While I like Lincoln in many ways and I like many of the people, that is partly a question of security, because I have known them for a long time. I find it lacking in stimulation in many ways. I am a musician by profession and qualification, and there is no concert hall in Lincoln. This tells you something about the cultural life of the city, which is pretty thin in my judgement. There are amateur orchestras, of course, and there is a professional choir in the sense of the Cathedral choir being professional, but there is no professional orchestra and there is no professional theatre company any longer. We have visits by the Hallé Orchestra once a year, but only in the Cathedral, and much as I love the Cathedral, it is a lousy concert hall because of the acoustics, and it is always cold. If you live in Lincolnshire and want cultural activity in your life, you have to go to Peterborough, Sheffield or London.

Lincoln in the past has produced sons who have gone on to be quite famous, but it has never ever been able to retain them because there is no tradition of culture here, except what is provided by the Cathedral. For instance, William Byrd was born here and was organist here, and Neville Mariner was born here, but both of them – just to take two examples in the musical world, and centuries apart – had to go away in order to realize their potential.

That brings me to another point. At the moment we have just one 125 rail service a day from Lincoln to London, and one back again. That is good, it has started in a very small way to put Lincoln on the map, but the real problem of this city is the fact that it is not that well known. There is an old joke in Lincoln that when you go to King's Cross and ask for a ticket to Lincoln, they say, 'Where?' The truth is that Lincoln has always been an 'isolated city'.

You have to remember how this city first came about. It occupies a strategic place topographically, in the sense that it sits on the top of a limestone ridge that runs virtually the whole length of the county like a spine and is breached in only one place, at Lincoln, where the River Witham flows through it. The Romans settled here because they saw it as a strategically important point, one that could be defended and around which a city could be built. They built a huge garrison, which needed to be fed, and even in Roman times there were surpluses of cereals in Lincolnshire.

So it came about that when Remigius, who was William the Conqueror's lieutenant and was largely responsible for putting the Domesday Book together, was sent by William to set up a new diocese somewhere in the northern half of what had previously been the diocese of Dorchester, it was not surprising that he should find himself in Lincoln. So Lincoln was simply the administrative centre for what is a huge agricultural area, nothing more than that.

It's a very isolated city, which is slowly undergoing change. But until we can get some decent communications, Lincoln will never be on the map, bearing in mind that in this county we have not one single mile of designated motorway, not one. We have got chunks of the A1, which pass through the south of the county, but they are not motorways. If we had a decent road link, it would quite certainly bring prosperity into this county and put us on the map. There is a fear, I know, that if you bring prosperity in, that same road will take people out. I don't think it will, because Lincolnshire has a quality of life that is the envy of many. The ever-spreading tentacles of the economic renaissance of the South-east have stretched now to the south of Lincolnshire; Stamford and Grantham are beginning to be very prosperous indeed. Grantham, of course, is on the electrified east coast main line, so its success is almost assured. Stamford is not quite as strategically placed, but on the doorstep of some gorgeous country where everybody wants to live.

More and more people are beginning to move into Lincoln to retire. There is relatively cheap housing at the moment, though house prices have shot up. House prices are still cheaper here than they are in the South-east. For many, the prospect of selling a house expensively in the South-east and moving to rural Lincolnshire where they can buy a house for half what they have sold their house in the south for, would enable them to live in certain comfort for the rest of their life, which is a very attractive proposition.

The Fabric Fund financially supports the work, maintenance and restoration of Lincoln Cathedral. Hugh of Avalon was asked to come here by Henry II to rebuild his Cathedral following the collapse in the earthquake of 1185, and that fund has been in existence ever since. By fabric I don't mean soft furnishings – I'm not talking about cassocks and surplices and frontals – but fabric in the sense of stone, wood, lead and glass. In modern practical terms, it is the administrative wing of the works department of the Cathedral.

The Fabric Fund supports a huge works department: we employ permanently, full time, stonemasons, plumbers, glaziers, carpenters, engineers – all the skills that are needed to maintain and repair the building day by day – and, of course, architects, clerks of work, plasterers, drivers and all the rest of it. We have an annual requirement for something like £300,000 a year, and my job is part fund-raising, part administrative, because we have a capital reserve, which has to be administered in terms of investments and so on. And because we perceive that fund-raising goes hand in hand with public relations, I am also public relations officer to the Dean and Chapter.

I am perfectly happy to spend most of my time on PR. Experience shows that we can concentrate on two syndromes of affection that exist within this county. I call them the 'welcoming beacon' and the 'it was a lovely service'. Bear in mind that as you approach Lincoln from as much as thirty miles away, you can see the Cathedral stuck on top of the hill. Lincolnians returning to Lincoln from a spell away see the Cathedral as they approach. It immediately has this welcoming beacon effect, and because home has a symbiosis with security and comfort, inevitably they see the Cathedral as part of this.

Most people in Lincoln also have been to a service in the Cathedral at one time or another; it may be one of the county services, the enthronement of a bishop, the ordination of a friend or relation, whatever. We are well aware of the fact that services are a form of dramatic presentation, a form of stage management. We spend hours thinking about how we are going to organize our major services: the numbers of people, the order in which events happen. It is all part of an act of great dramatic effect done for the purposes of uplifting the spirits of the faithful as an aid to their worship of God – we do not provide the trappings and the processions as an offering to God *per se*.

The combination of fabulous architecture, fabulous craftsmanship, fabulous music, fabulous ritual, all of that produces a wealth of emotional feeling towards the Cathedral, and people take away a precious memory. So it is really these two emotions that we appeal to when we tell people what a marvellous place the Cathedral is.

We support the maintenance and restoration work to the tune of £300,000 per year, and the Church Commissioners put in something like £50,000. The Church of England is quite a wealthy Church, but don't underestimate its expenses – they are huge.

We own all the buildings immediately around the Cathedral, which is a fantastic series of houses, virtually priceless in terms of our national heritage. But because the maintenance and restoration of those houses is an enormously expensive business, and because of Lincoln's remoteness, we can't attract really wealthy people to live in them who could afford to pay huge rents, so we don't actually have that good a return on them.

For the day-to-day running expenses – paying for the heating system, paying the vergers' wages, paying for the tuning of the organ, paying for the stipends of some of the clergy – it is to those expenses, broadly speaking, that the visitors to the Cathedral contribute.

I know it's controversial to charge visitors to come into a church, but we don't actually charge an entrance fee; we invite you to make a contribution. If you say, 'I have just come to say my prayers', that is fine, you may come in to say your prayers, no one will try to take money off you. But the other side of that coin is that you can say your prayers without coming in.

Joe Public perfectly happily pays to go and look at a castle or a country house, or to watch motor racing. Ninety per cent of the people who come to the Cathedral are coming to look at a chunk of heritage, not to look at it as a place of worship or a house of God. If that is the way they see it, there is no earthly reason why they shouldn't be asked to pay a quid towards the maintenance, is there? Anyway what is a quid? Good Lord, it's peanuts these days.

Money really is as much a guiding factor in the running of a cathedral as it is in any business. The East Midlands electricity board isn't charitable to us about the electric light that we burn in the Cathedral, or the oil company about the oil for the heating. And the Chapter has a perception of the way it wants the Cathedral to be run. That is fine, but every time you bring a consultant in or you ask someone to do a job, he has to be paid; no one works for charity, do they? I expect to be paid. I have to keep a motor car if they want me trailing around. My road tax costs £100 just like yours. Who is going to pay it?

Most cathedrals have had panic appeals within the last few years, virtually all of them; think of Salisbury, Winchester, Chichester, Ely, Wells, Peterborough, Ripon, York for a specific purpose, Hereford, Worcester, Exeter. There is no cause for complacency, because there is still plenty to do, but the fact remains that our Cathedral is weather- and water-tight, and because we have got our own permanent work-force constantly going round the Cathedral, we have never actually got to the stage where we have to say 'Help'.

I think that Lincoln is arguably the finest cathedral in England. There is an atmosphere in the choir at Lincoln that has to be experienced to be believed. People have been worshipping God in that place for 900 years – and it feels like it. It certainly has the finest site of any cathedral in this country. I know that people will tell one that it is rivalled by Durham, and I agree that within the context of the city Durham is a superb site, but it is only visible from quite a short distance away because the hills are all about; Lincoln is visible from all over this county. I drive 30,000 miles a year through this diocese talking to groups about the Cathedral. I come back towards Lincoln night after night, and I can tell you from which point in every direction you can first see the Cathedral on a clear night, and it is awesome.

I think the Cathedral is a fantastic piece of architecture, a fantastic piece of design, a fantastic tribute to the vision of former generations – but I don't think that my faith is dependent on the Cathedral, to be quite honest. There are times when I feel that the Church of England, with its constant difficulties and the frankly amorphous nature it has at the moment, there are times when I become very impatient of that and I feel that the Church of England gets in the way of my religion, and perhaps my religion gets in the way of my faith. But my faith is unshaken.

DULCIE DUKE, HISTORIAN

I WAS teaching in Virginia, but although I was very happy and I had made a great many friends, I didn't think that life in America for an unmarried woman was on. It is much better in England, and so I came home. I went to Crewe as a lecturer. One of my colleagues, who was in the art department, came over and said, 'The senior history lecturer at Lincoln is getting married. Why don't you apply for the post?' So I came over and visited Lincoln.

I saw the Cathedral standing on its hill, and it looked like a cat, with the two twin towers as the pricked ears. You know when a cat curls its tail round it, the tip stands up sometimes? That was the central tower. And it had got a cat's smile on its face. The city was only very small and sort of huddled on the slope, and the Cathedral was the cat watching over it.

The thing that astonished me, when I walked up the hill, was how the materials for that building were brought together and assembled. Of course, it took 200 years to get more or less what we see today, but it was all unmechanized: this mass of material had been collected by just sheer human power up the hill; it was such an achievement. The first period of building was the Norman Conquest, and it struck me that here the foreign lords had come and in an unfriendly neighbourhood they had established a stronghold, not so much for themselves, but for the glory of God, a sort of spiritual stronghold.

Going into the Cathedral, there was just so much space, there was a real feeling as if all the power of God and his angels was holding the fabric up and apart, otherwise the whole thing would come crashing in . . . It was a sunny day, winter-time, and I wandered round and I felt the city, and I applied and I got the job. That was in January 1952.

When I retired, I had worn a little rut in the city: I went to certain shops, and I went to certain places, and I knew certain churches. My parents were dead and my home had gone, and there was no reason to try to get back to Devon, so I decided I would live here.

At a time of personal difficulty I was taking a party of students to the Cathedral. My father had just died and I had some personal, private anxieties, and just inside the great West Door I looked round, and on a chair, an ordinary wooden chair leaned against the wall, there was a notice. I don't know why it was there, or what it was, but it was a great help. It was lettered, in quite big letters, 'TRUST GOD'. Whenever I go into the Cathedral – and I worship there now since I live just a few hundred yards from it – I am reminded of those words, and I am thrilled and restored and uplifted, although depressed with my own failure to live up to the standards.

I regard the Cathedral as a great comfort. I know that all sorts of evil and terrible things have been done all over the world, and they're being done in the name of religion, but there's still, I feel, a core of sanity surviving while the Cathedral stands.

I usually sit on the north side of the choir, because I have Parkinson's Disease, so I find walking and climbing steps a bit difficult. I sit as close to the chancel rail area as I can. If I look up, I see the eleventh angel, with the hawk on his wrist, and it always reminds me that religion is not all to do with sanctimonious sins and sadness, but it is for the enjoyment of God's world, which includes hawks.

This Cathedral embodies the history of England. It was built by Remigius at the orders of William the Conqueror, who, sadly, never got as far as Lincoln. I don't think William II came, but Henry I did. Stephen certainly was here: it was here that he lost his crown three times in the Cathedral, which was supposed to portend that his son wouldn't succeed him as king. Matilda was here; she fled from the castle in the snow, draped in a sheet. Her son, Henry II, came to Lincoln. Richard the Lionheart didn't come, but John came, and he carried St Hugh's body to his tomb. That's depicted in the Great Window; he is one of the four kings carrying St Hugh's body. Henry III was very much involved in the building of Westminster Abbey, and although he gave the writ that allowed the Angel Choir to be built, I don't think he ever came to see the result.

Edward I came, of course, because of the burial of his wife, Eleanor of Castile – her tomb is the one under the East Window. Edward was on his way to Scotland. Because Eleanor had been ill, she was to join the King at Lincoln, and she was coming by easy stages. But the illness developed again and she died at Harby, near Lincoln. The King made a breakneck journey to try to get to her – he was very much in love with his wife – but he was too late, the roads . . . well, even now, it's a side road to Harby and you have to cross the Trent, and there was no bridge at that time. He was heart-broken. Her body was embalmed and her viscera were buried in the Angel Choir in the Cathedral, and the King ordered a tomb to be made over her viscera. Her body was moved to London, and everywhere they had to stop the night a marvellous, fantastic cross was erected to mark her resting place, and there were twelve Eleanor crosses, the last of which was Charing Cross.

Edward II must have come, because his father presented him as the first English Prince of Wales in 1301 in the Chapter House. Edward III was actually in Lincoln with his mother, Isabella, when his father was assassinated. Edward III was succeeded by Richard II because Edward III's heir, the Black Prince, died before he did. Richard was succeeded by Henry IV, and he must have come because he gave a charter. His son, Henry V, probably didn't come, because he died young, and Henry VI, I don't think he came.

Edward IV certainly came, to both the city and the Cathedral, because he was trying to raise money on his way to Yorkshire, where there was a great battle. There were wild roses growing in the hedgerows and, to distinguish his supporters, they picked white roses and stuck them in their caps. Edward, who was then Duke of York, was acclaimed king at the age of 19 after he overthrew Henry VI at the bitterly fought battle of Towton in 1461. The battles that followed that constitute the Wars of the Roses. I don't suppose his son, Edward V, came, and I don't think Richard III had time to come; he was devoted to York anyway.

There had been an attempt to displace Henry VII. It was the young man who had the title the Earl of Lincoln who raised the rebellion in Lincoln, and there was a battle. That failed and Henry VII came – it was a punitive exercise, just to make sure that things were organized after that abortive rebellion – but he only stayed a very short time.

Henry VIII came. It was here that his last wife but one, Catherine Howard, misconducted herself with Thomas Culpepper, in the bishop's own palace. Cranmer, the old goat, told the King. So she was executed, and so was Culpepper. And the King wept for 'his rose without a thorn'. I think it's most terrible of Cranmer to sneak on them. Nothing to do with him. But Henry was by that time very badly crippled with this ulcerated leg, and so I don't suppose he was able to get out and about much, and the Queen was very young . . .

Henry VIII was succeeded by his son, Edward VI, who didn't come, but his daughter, Elizabeth, came. They used to move from manor to manor and eat up the supplies, leave the place filthy and move on to the next. I suppose Lincoln was as good a place to stay as any. Elizabeth did give this beautiful charter, which gave the city certain rights: exemption from taxes, they could hold their own courts and all sorts of other privileges.

After Elizabeth you have James I, who certainly stopped here – he went hunting on Dunston Heath. Charles I didn't come to Lincoln; I think the nearest was Nottingham.

And then there was the Commonwealth. I don't think Cromwell came, but certainly the parliamentarian troops were here – they knocked the Cathedral to bits. As you might know, the best guns at that time were made partly of brass, which was the best metal. So they ripped up all the beautiful brasses in the Cathedral, where they were encamped literally, horses and everything, in the nave. Four hundred and something brasses they took, they tore the brass gates off the choir – they took eight barge-loads of brass from the Cathedral in three days of systematic looting, and sold them in London. What else they took I don't know, but they knocked the heads off the little saints on the screen, used them as target practice. They destroyed the bishop's tomb in the south transept on the right-hand side. It was made of silver and all you've got left now are two little supporting pillars. And they took some of the bells – bell metal was also very valuable.

Charles II came, and he gave the right to hold horse races here – the Lincoln Handicap – and he gave a cup. From Charles II's visit until very recently the Lincoln Handicap opened the flat-racing season. I used to go every year, but now it's moved to Doncaster I don't bother.

After Charles II, James II, and I'm sure he didn't come. Then William and Mary, and, try as I might, I can't find that they ever came because William was too busy in Europe.

Queen Anne, I'm sure she didn't come. George I, I don't think he came, nor did George II, or George III or IV. William IV was succeeded by Victoria, and she came with Prince Albert, and there was tremendous rejoicing in the city.

Edward VII used to come to the races. He came at least twice; I'm not sure that he didn't come more often. He got a bad press. I know he had girl-friends, and he went racing and gambling, but his mother and father didn't give him any chance to get to grips with any sort of profession. When he was a very young man he wanted to be in the army, and the Queen absolutely refused that. I'm rather sorry for Edward VII. He's like the Parable of the Talents: he buried his talents and paid the penalty.

George V came. The Cathedral was in a terrible state of disrepair at that time. Dean Fry tried to enlist rich people's support for the Cathedral, and he thought the only way to do it was to get the King to come. People were such snobs, he thought, they would come. So Dean Fry started a society called

The Friends of the Cathedral, and the King and Queen were the first two friends. People rushed to join then, there was a great luncheon and a 'to-doment', and people were presented to the King. Dean Fry was the first man to think of asking Americans to support the Cathedral, and he went to America with an appeal.

George V was succeeded by Edward VIII, who came as Prince of Wales and was accorded a welcome that I would class as modified rapture. Then his brother, George VI, came with his wife, Queen Elizabeth, now the Queen Mother.

I saw the present Queen each time she came. The last time she came, which was 1980, to mark the 700th anniversary of the building of the Angel Choir, it poured with rain; it always does, it seems to me, when she comes here. She was wearing a most beautiful scarlet cloth coat and a little black velvet cap. And, as you know, she's small and slim, got very pretty feet and ankles. The umbrella that was held over her was not really adequate, but she went round the Cathedral smiling, and she did a walkabout. I longed to ask her, 'Your Majesty, did you choose your scarlet coat because it's the scarlet cloth that Lincoln produced, which only royalty and bishops and archbishops might wear?' But I hadn't the neck to ask her.

The first time she came here was when they opened Pelham Bridge, in 1953 or 1954. It was pouring with rain and they were having a 'do'. But Her Majesty was actually in the pouring rain without even the vestige of an umbrella, much less a raincoat. She wore very pretty pale grey court shoes and gloves, and a grey hat with pink in it, and they turned black with the rain. She came to the football ground, with terrible soggy puddles. They could have put straw down for her to walk on, but they made no attempt and she splashed nobly through the puddles to the stand and the directors' box. All the civic dignitaries were lined up in the pouring rain, heads of schools and various people, and presented to her by the former Lord-Lieutenant, who I don't think knew t'other from which . . . all in the pouring rain. I felt so sorry for her. And shortly afterwards she got laryngitis. I swear it was the cold and the wet, because she spent at least two hours with not an umbrella in sight.

Prince Charles was at Cranwell, and he's come to Lincoln several times to raise money for the Cathedral, concerts and so on. I've got all sorts of soft spots for him. When he was a boy at Cranwell, I was teaching, and it must have been a Saturday: I was walking up the Bail and I saw a beautiful Aston Martin sports car parked by the kerb, a dark blue one, and a young man with an open-necked shirt and bare head was sitting in the driver's seat talking to a much older man on the pavement. I thought, 'What a super car,' and then I looked at the young man, the driver, and I thought, 'I know him . . .' I thought, 'Oh dear, I'm terrible at forgetting my students' names,' and looked back over my shoulder and then realized it was the Prince of Wales! He saw that I recognized him and he did a little sort of wave. It was very nice of him. And then he came on an official visit to the Cathedral, something to do with the RAF, and there was a service. He was the most important person present, of course, and he's been several times more.

I don't know if you saw a television programme called *A Vision of Britain* that he did? I was so thrilled by what he said that I took my courage in both my hands and wrote to him and said, 'Congratulations'. And I got a charming letter back from Kensington Palace thanking me for my encouragement. Don't you think that was nice, to take the trouble to thank me for my letter? I think he will make a good king when his time comes. And I don't think he will forget Lincoln.

THE VERY REVEREND HONOURABLE OLIVER TWISLETON-WYKEHAM-FIENNES, RETIRING DEAN

I CAME from a slightly church background, you might say; great-grandfather was a clergyman, and we've always been church-goers, classic English, wouldn't-think-of-not-going-to-church.

I think that vocation is best described as a niggle, a sort of persistent niggle that you can't ignore. I think if one is finding oneself thinking about the way one is, and actually thinking of God as real and significant, one had better do something about it. But one doesn't plan it, it doesn't work like that – the blinding flash, St Paul and all that caper – that wasn't me at all. If I was starting today, I would probably have fetched up as a social worker. It was a sense of service, I think.

The first time I saw Lincoln, I was stationed at Ranby camp, which is over Newark way. A friend of mine had an ancient open MG and some petrol. Four of us cramped into this thing and we drove here for the first Remembrance Day Service after the war. It really was very extraordinary. We only just managed to squeeze in at the back, standing room only – there were no chairs left in the place, it was absolutely packed from wall to wall. Quite frightening. I've seen 7,000 people there, but I guess there were probably 10,000 or 12,000 and I do remember very distinctly having that shivers-down-the-spine feeling.

How do you come to this sort of job? You get a letter from, in my case, Harold Wilson, asking would you like to be Dean in Lincoln? It was a very curious appointment. Deans are normally old, it's a very top job, and it's a scholar's job, it's a musician's job, and I was none of those things. What I was, I suppose, was a successful, if you can use the word, parish priest. I think what happened was that the Bishop identified the fact that what this Cathedral needed was somebody who had those skills.

Lincoln had a reputation of being conservative and isolated, perhaps even unfriendly. There was no place for women in the Cathedral much: they weren't allowed to sit in the canon stalls, there was no question of a women's ministry. It was a highly traditional, enclosed cathedral at a time when lots of things were changing in the late sixties.

There was trouble early on. I wanted to do things, like using the modern forms of services, and some of the older clergy disapproved. There were sermons saying the new dean is doing the wrong thing, and those sort of attacks. I'm quite sensitive. It hurt. But I have always believed the Christian tradition is one of change. All the things that we do – baptism and confirmation and so on – are about change, and if you're going to be traditional in a building like this, you actually have to change all the time. If you look at it architecturally, until the nineteenth century, there is no single piece of architecture here that wasn't, in its day, utterly modern. And they really stretched out to be modern; it's the glass-and-steel of its day all the way through. In 1072 it was highly modern, and in 1192 it was highly modern; even Wren goes and puts in an absolute classic 1674 building into the middle of the Gothic. That's the right tradition – it's fundamental to Christianity – and that had been lost. I think it's taken us a long time to get closer.

The Dean and Chapter is the sole decision-making place. Quite rightly. I think authority has to be bedded into a central committee. The difficulty of being a reforming dean, which I was, is that you have to do it by consensus. You have four other clergymen, and change can be made only by a majority. Now that's fine, and consensus is a good thing, but looking over twenty years of being Dean, I think one would have liked to have made more changes. But there are now women ministers of all sorts, and much more freedom for women in the building;

there are shops – a gift shop, a coffee shop; there is involvement of the congregation; there is more involvement in the city, that sort of thing. What has also changed, I think importantly, is that the place is much more approachable and friendly.

I was sometimes not at all sure that Christianity needs this sort of building. But I do actually now believe, as I didn't when I came here, that this Cathedral and the others are a major missionary opportunity, an opportunity to proclaim Christianity. And I think we've succeeded in doing that – I do think the house has been put in order and we're now ready to receive guests.

There have been many moments of splendour in there: I think of the enthronement of our Bishop, Christmas Eve services, Remembrance Day, of course, where you've really felt that the building was helping you to do the job. There are certain things that you can do only in a great building like this. These massive services, if you get them right, make people realize that they're not isolated as Christians.

The most fascinating question is why they built these enormous, vast buildings. I think they did have a great picture of the majesty of God and they were reaching up to express this, but in 1072, when building started, they were the conquerors, they were the invaders, and they did destroy something like 10 per cent of the population's houses to put it up, so that's not a good start. But I think they must have had some sense of the beauty and majesty of God, and they certainly had this need to have a central point of prayer in a Christian community.

Neither God nor the Christian faith changes. What does change is human understanding of it, and in different periods of history, different emphases come to the fore. At the moment we are going through a period when the concepts of majesty and strength and grandeur are being traded for community and love in the small scale, which are quite difficult to communicate through that building. But if you come to some of our early morning services, or our 9.30 service on a Sunday morning, we actually do a great deal in terms of speaking of the simplicity of Christianity, despite the building.

I'm actually worried. It looks like we're heading for a period when there is going to be a whole lot of rigidity. It seems to be happening in Judaism, it's clearly happening in American Christianity and it's happening in Islam. What frightens me is that we're beginning to hear people say, 'Unless you think like I think, you're not a Christian', or you're not a Jew or a Muslim, or whatever. It's very odd and very frightening, because at the heart of Christianity is grace, and grace means freedom.

I do not believe that what *I* have as my Christian faith is necessarily right; it's right for me, it's as right as I can get it, but I wouldn't dream of saying it is right for everybody.

One of the most neglected Christian attributes is hope, and what one hopes for here, given 1½ million people walking through these doors every year, is that you are providing something so that when they leave, they are moved towards what is good – and this building does move people.

I've now made the decision to leave. I came here committed to do five years and no more, and never found the right moment to leave. I think I probably ought to have left about three or four years ago. I suspect that this place needs a younger man. I'm getting on, I'm 62, that's past the time when ordinary people make bright, vigorous decisions. I've had too many heart attacks and I've slowed down – if you get swished off to hospital, it's silly not to.

We're going to live at Colsterworth, about forty miles south. Well, you couldn't sit around here and breathe down your successor's neck, could you? You see, one of the things about being a dean, particularly in a country like this, is that you are very much a persona; I mean the dean is 'The Dean' whether you like it or not. And English life is still a society of which the Church of England is part – bishops in the House of Lords and all that; in fact, the Mayor is the first citizen and I am the second citizen of this city. I'm actually in favour of all that because I don't think that anybody has produced a better pattern. There are moments when I think I do no more here than pretending to be squire of a village, but, as a matter of fact, I actually think a good squire makes a lot of difference to the village.

I know why I'm in the business of being a priest is because I do believe in God, and I believe more in God now than I did when I started.

THE RIGHT REVEREND BOB HARDY, BISHOP OF LINCOLN

WHEN I was a schoolboy, we came from the grammar school in Wakefield to do a history project, and I first saw it then; I'd be about 14. Lincoln was an amazing contrast to Wakefield, which is a parish church cathedral, and a lovely building in its way, but the position of Lincoln and the whole massiveness of that West Front is amazing. It's an overwhelming building, isn't it; an extraordinary building.

I suppose I come from a very ordinary middle-class background. My father's a retired accountant, I'm a grammar-school boy, and I went to Cambridge. I come from a Christian background, but not in any way a clerical background. My grandfather, a retired railway signalman, was a church warden and a very faithful Christian. He had a very deep Christian influence on me, I think because he was one of these very rare people who was transparently good, and even as a child I realized that he was a good man. I've met quite a few good people and they've all been influential, but he was recognizably the first, and therefore that much more powerful.

I'm the sort of person that's always been a part of the Church, but I tried to test out these feelings all the way through: sixth form at school, National Service, the first couple of years at Cambridge. I had a kind of inner compulsion to test it, which in a way has never really left me. I continuously looked to see if there was an alternative to becoming a priest – alternative jobs, alternative truths, alternative ways of looking at things.

I tried to broaden my Christian experience to find where on the kind of Christian spectrum I happened to be. For instance, I used to go regularly to a Pentecostal church, and I began to realize the variety of ways in which people come to know God and worship him. I've found my way, but I recognize that there are many other ways that have an integrity to them.

I think most people, if they're honest, are a bit ambivalent about the Church. I think you can be appalled by its worldliness and its apparent compromise, and some of its darker sides, and I think sensible people ought to test it all the time. I'm still testing it in some ways.

But the feeling that one ought to be ordained never went away. My father kept open the partnership in his accountancy practice for a long time, not necessarily in the hope that I would follow him, but so I could have the possibility. But I kept coming back to the feeling that I ought to be ordained, that this is what God wanted.

I had a spiritual experience in Hereford Cathedral when I was doing National Service in the RAF. I had a sort of disclosure of God's presence with me and His reality to me, and I think that was a real turning point. It's never happened since, but in a sense it doesn't need to, because it happened and I know it's real. If you say to me, 'Tell me about the service', I couldn't, but I could point to you now where I sat: it was half-way down the choir on the right-hand side facing the altar. Nothing happened really, that was the amazing part about it. I just felt that God knew me and that I knew He was real, that He was there and that He was what I had understood Him to be through my faith, and that there was to be real fulfilment in that relationship.

I was a bit overwhelmed by it, I'm bound to say, and I did try to savour it, although it didn't stay very long. But it stayed long enough for me to know that it was absolutely real, and it was of such a kind that it actually fitted in with the record of other people's experiences of God as I had read it in scripture, which was a great comfort. I could then understand something about Isaiah in the Temple or Jeremiah feeling that he was known in his mother's womb.

Nevertheless I've never had a particularly serene faith. I've never had a lengthy period of un-faith, but I've certainly gone through periods of doubt, and I find my faith very severely tested from time to time even now. I mean, there's a particular problem with a family of one of my clergy that I find desperately difficult to understand, someone whose son has got leukaemia at the age of 21. I'm devastated by this. I look at my own children, and as they get older, in a sense it almost makes this other family's tragedy seem crueller; I think inevitably you ask questions. I'm going to see one of the deaconesses in the diocese this very afternoon; she's got a cancer and I worry about her.

In a curious sort of way, I think what affirms my faith is the faithfulness of other people. And I think my faith's affirmed by the beauty of the world. My faith's affirmed by the Cathedral, too, in a way. You can't go into the Cathedral without being inspired by the sheer human achievement of it. There's not a week goes by without I go into the Cathedral for one reason or another, even if it's only to walk through it, and I think it's enormously inspiring; first of all because it's so very beautiful, and then I think it's inspiring for what it represents, I mean as a statement of faith. It may be a statement of faith from the past, but for someone to put up the highest building in Europe, which it was for many centuries, is a huge statement of faith. You can't walk around the Cathedral without being buffeted by wind, even on the stillest sort of day, and yet that place has stood there for centuries. It's amazing.

I never really thought about a career; things sort of happened around me. I started off on a housing estate in Manchester, and then I got an offer to go as a college chaplain to Cambridge, and that was an opportunity to teach. I think a lot of clergy have a hankering after an academic position, as if it's a kind of superior sort of life, but I realized soon after I got there, in a matter of weeks, that my heart was really in a parish, that I wanted to go back to a parish, and that is what I did. In a sense I've never applied for a job, except when my bishop ordered me to apply for a job, and my career has just sort of taken care of itself.

Lincoln came into my life in a brown paper envelope from the Prime Minister asking if she could put my name forward to the Queen. I'd no inkling this was on the cards.

The awkwardness was that I couldn't tell anyone until it was public because one has to keep these appointments under wraps for some time. I had the letter about the middle of July and the thing wasn't announced until September, although I obviously talked it through with my wife. My son found out about it because he was poking around my desk for some tape, and he shouted out, 'Dad, you've had a letter from the Prime Minister!' I told him then, and we also told my other son and daughter. They came to Lincoln and had a look at the Bishop's House through the gate, and brought me back a guide book, one of those Lincoln Cathedral booklets. I didn't dare come in case anybody identified me and wondered what I was doing there.

When you have to move, there are all sorts of practical problems: dates, schools, wife's job – my wife's a doctor – the house. You're into the practicalities of the thing and how you're going to manage, so in a way the romance of the place didn't feature too highly at the beginning. But being an historian, there is a kind of historical romance to me. I find it deeply moving to read about some of my predecessors and to know that I hold the same office as the man who built Lincoln Cathedral. You do feel if you're the seventieth Bishop of Lincoln, as I am, a lot of people have given their life and their energies to Lincoln, and it's good to be a part of that chain.

My favourite bishop in a way is the other Robert Lincoln, Robert Sanderson, who actually spent forty years as vicar of a tiny Lincolnshire village called Boothby Pagnell before he became Bishop of Lincoln. I think of him ministering away to his people all through the years of the Civil War, and then popping up here.

There's a lovely book about former bishops of Lincoln with a chapter on each bishop, and I often read it, because it's good reading. I'll show it to you. Page 284 . . . let's see, he was only Bishop of Lincoln for two and a half years, '1660 to 1663 . . . born in Rotherham', he was a Yorkshireman like me, you see. 'He was presented to the vicarage of Wyberton and then he went to Boothby Pagnell, near Grantham, and held the office there and contributed to the Book of Common Prayer', so he's

Restoration. 'Sanderson was raised to the seat of Lincoln on the recommendation of Gilbert Sheldon, then Bishop of London . . . Though Sanderson was 73, he was an active as well as a learned bishop. He was kind to Nonconformists and if he had had his way he would have been more lenient than the law permitted.'

He wasn't a famous Bishop of Lincoln, but he was a remarkable contributor to Anglican life. He was one of the Caroline divines, he wrote about theology and he was interested in the early Church and the early Church fathers. And in a way he kind of steadied the ship at a time when religion in this country was in a pretty volatile state.

Of course, the diocese was bigger then, much bigger. Through the Middle Ages it gradually became reduced, but it was still a very considerable diocese when Sanderson was around. He ran the diocese largely through archdeacons, who went around the place and kept an eye on things, and, of course, if you don't have telephones and letters, you've actually got quite a lot of leisure; you don't even attempt to do certain things. He wouldn't get fussed about, as I do, trying to go to Mablethorpe to launch a lifeboat in an afternoon, and come back and do something else in the evening; he just wouldn't do that. And, by and large, he didn't have to worry about money, because virtually every parish was self-supporting, and you can get on with all sorts of things if you're not interfered with.

I'm not responsible for the Cathedral's organization. The relationship is curious really, because in a sense it's my base, it's where I put my bottom down in the end and it's where I draw a lot of my sustenance and inspiration from. I try to celebrate most weeks in the Cathedral. I try to walk in there once a week; the staff are very kind to me, from the Dean onwards, and they are very affectionate and make me feel a part of them. I've got my seat there: my cathedra, the Bishop's throne. It's a carved stall at the end of the choir opposite the pulpit. It's a bit grand, but it's very comfortable and I like sitting in it! It's very important occasionally to actually feel like a bishop, and I don't often feel like a bishop.

JENNIFER HARVEY
DEAN'S SECRETARY

I'M from Brant Broughton. It's twelve miles door-to-door from home to the Deanery.

I've always been involved with the Church from as long as I can remember, always gone to church, to Sunday school. The church is quite an important part of your life in a village. And the Cathedral was just somewhere that I came to once every so often, perhaps with visitors or on a day's outing or something. But it was always there on the top of the hill, and you can see it from Brant Broughton, even at night you can see it, because it's floodlit. I never ever dreamt that I would work here.

Brant Broughton has one of the nicest country village churches, a large church with a very tall, elegant spire, and it is noted as a beautiful church. It had a bit of controversy about fifteen years ago because the picture over the altar was discovered to be worth, then, £40,000, and there was a great argument about whether we should keep it or sell it. It ended with a visit to the Cathedral, because there was a church court case over it and at that time what is now the Cathedral shop was the Consistory Court, and that was where those sort of cases were heard. A lot of us came to court just because we'd never been to anything like that before. That was when Brant Broughton was put on the map; well, perhaps not on the map exactly, but it was quite a big affair for a small village, only 500 or 600 people, to discover that their painting is worth a fortune. We've still got it and it's there at our church.

I've been working here five years come this November. I went to work in London for a year. I did like London, but I would have liked it better if I could have got home at weekends a bit more. I came back and ended up working at the Lincoln Co-operative Society, which I wasn't really all that excited about to begin with, but, as it turned out, it was a jolly interesting job. I was secretary to the chief executive, and I stayed there until I came here. I'd no intentions of leaving until I saw a job advertised in the *Echo*. It had hardly any detail to it at all; it could have been anything really. And I thought, 'Oh, it's time I had a change.' I was advised by lots of people that I was probably doing the wrong thing, and it would be very quiet and not half as interesting as where I was.

I suppose I took a chance really, because I could have left my job at the Co-op and regretted it. But I just felt that this was where I wanted to work. I nearly gave up because I didn't hear anything for so long. Then I got a letter on my birthday, saying would I come for an interview, and I got the job.

They were shocked at the Co-op; they all thought I was a fixture. Quite honestly, some of them thought I was pulling their legs when I said I was leaving. When people stay over a certain time, and I'd been there in the teens of years, they do think you're not going to move, don't they? *I* didn't think I was going to move! But I've never regretted it for one minute, oh no. It was the right move.

I didn't know the Dean personally, but he'd preached at Brant Broughton, and if you're involved with the Church in any way, you know who everyone is, and he'd come to preach at our Harvest Festival. In fact – I've told him about this since – if I hear a poem, or a talk or something, and it registers, I try to make a little note of it in a diary. His sermon, the one he preached for that Harvest Festival, which was seven or eight years before I came to work here – I looked back through this book when I came to work here, and I'd written down what he preached about. He'd made an impact, you see. He does make an impact, because his sermons are direct and to the point.

Working for the Dean takes up a lot of time, and as Chapter Secretary, I also prepare the agendas for the Chapter meetings, and go to the meetings, which are jolly interesting, and do the minutes. I laugh to myself at these meetings because you get five people who speak so eloquently; they put arguments forward and they disagree just like anyone – and probably disagree more than people imagine – but they always come out with a solution at the end of the day.

I also do the Events List. You've seen how many events are going on – Cathedral concerts and special services and all this sort of thing – so when people want to hold events, they must ring or write. We have a little Events Committee, of which I'm the Secretary, along with Roy, the head verger. Between us we look after the bookings in the Cathedral, sorting out when people can come, and then I send out confirmations. That's quite a job.

The Dean's a super boss, he really is, he couldn't be nicer. He's very kind, and I'm sure he makes himself busier by the fact that he will never refuse to see anybody; he just pushes his paperwork aside. In fact, the first thing he told me when I came here is that papers are not important but people are, so that if people want to see him, the paperwork can be done anytime. That's why he often works very late into the night.

I suppose for the majority of people who come to the Cathedral, it's a place to visit just like they'd visit anywhere else; but at the heart of it is this cycle of prayer that goes on every day. At the end of the day it's the religious side of the place that's the most important. Come what may, there'll be matins said every day, and evensong said every day; it doesn't matter if there's nobody there. I'm sure people don't realize that. It could be the depths of winter on an awful day, and there may be only two people in the congregation, but members of Chapter are still there.

Mid- to late afternoon in the winter or early spring, you can go in and there's not a soul around. It's very dark and all the visitors have gone; it's like being at the seaside in the wintertime, it's quite a different feeling.

I go to my own church at Brant Broughton on a Sunday. We pray for the Cathedral because it is the centre of the Church in Lincolnshire, and that's rather nice; I feel proud. I know that sounds silly, but it is a privilege to be able to work here.

Nearly everybody in Lincolnshire has an affection for the Cathedral, perhaps because it's on a hill and so many people can see it. Everybody who drives into Lincoln can see it from – I don't know what the farthest distance is – a terrific long way. It stands out so proudly as a sort of beacon, a landmark. I think it is very important to people in Lincolnshire, even though they may not have any close religious ties with it. If it were to be damaged or if anything were to happen to it, I think they would rally round immediately because it's part of their lives. They're very proud of it.

I try not to think about the Dean leaving. I know he's going, but I can't quite accept it. I'm very sorry really. I'm pleased for him and Mrs Fiennes, I'm sure that it's the right stage for them to go, but I can't imagine the place, after all that time, without him. I don't think anyone can really.

JOHN HARVEY, STEWARD

I'M an East Yorkshireman; in other words I was born within sight of Lincolnshire. The first time I saw Lincoln Cathedral, I was with my father. I must have been youngish, in my late teens, I suppose . . . Yes, either very late teens or 21, 22, something like that. And the abiding memory I have is going into a little chapel, which I now know was the Longman Chapel, and for some reason, for a short space of time Magna Carta was housed in that Chapel, in a great big safe with a spotlight on it.

My father was tremendously interested in churches – he was a historian – and as children we made jokes about it and hated all that sort of thing. We were a great big family of six and he was a gentle man, and we made fun of him all the time. I only wish he could see me now. I'd give anything for him to see me now doing this lot.

Anyway, I went into this chapel, and to my absolute astonishment I realized there was Magna Carta, and I'd no idea it was even there. Just to walk in and look at it, that took my breath away, because father had given me what might be called a translation of Magna Carta, and pointed out to me at least two incredible clauses in it that were so wise that they summed up the whole essence of law and justice and English fairness.

There was one particular phrase that hammered itself into my mind; it was 'that no one . . .', oh dear, wait a moment, my memory's going all the time these days. 'No one shall . . . no one shall withhold the right' or 'no one shall imprison' or is it 'no one shall withhold the liberty of anybody'? It's one sentence that sums up the entire law of civilized nations. Your readers can look it up, can't they?

I spent forty years of my life in London in advertising and marketing, and loved every minute of it, it was my life. Then I did a foolish thing when I was in my late fifties: I helped to start up a little company, which was marvellous for eighteen months and then fell flat on its face. I lost every halfpenny I had and I had no pension at all. My wife and I looked at each other and said, 'What the hell are we going to do?' I had a little cottage in Italy, a tiny little peasant cottage – well, it was four walls and a roof and nothing else, but we had made it into something with our own hands, and my wife, to my astonishment, said, 'Let's go and live in Italy.' So we packed up our furniture, gave half of it away, and the other half we took to Italy, and we lived there for five years.

Marvellous five years, not quite so for my wife. She didn't take to the language. Barbara was by nature a person who was lacking confidence, insecure. She didn't take to the language as I did. My friends had said, 'You'll be all right, plenty of people can speak English in Italy.' Not in Umbria they don't; not halfway up a mountain side they don't! Of course, I just like communicating, so I was all right. I had the country, I had a vineyard and olive trees, and love doing things with my hands. But Barbara didn't drive a car, so she was lonely, and that's why she was glad to come back.

I got a letter one day from my son, who was also in marketing and who had finally decided he was going to cut out the whole of the nonsense of boardroom stabs in the back and do what he'd always dreamt of doing, and that was running a restaurant. Knowing I liked using my hands, he said in this letter, 'If you think you could come back for a couple of months, Dad, I could do with your help.' This was a gift from heaven for my wife, so we came straight back here, helped him set the place up, and bought a tiny, tiny terraced house down the road, and that's how I came to live in Lincoln.

In fact, my wife's mother was born here. Barbara remembered the Cathedral, she remembered everything, so it was absolutely lovely for her. The last four years of her life, she was happier than she had ever been before. She was immediately involved with the restaurant; together we decorated the entire place. But I was frequently up at the Cathedral because I became a steward, and she was left on her own again, so she had to find something to do. She said, 'I want to do something in the Cathedral,' which she loved. 'I'm not clever enough to do the flowers,' she said; 'I couldn't be a guide or anything like that' – and I remember these were her exact words – 'Do you think they'd let me clean the brasses?' I said, 'Let you? Let you? You must be joking!' She took over the responsibility of cleaning all the brasses in the Cathedral, and she did that the whole of her time here.

She is very, very fondly remembered by everyone, so that when she died – very suddenly, which is a marvellous way to go – and I talked to dear old Bill Dudman, who was Christopher's predecessor as archdeacon, and I said, 'I don't know, Bill, about your feelings on this, but she loved the Cathedral so . . .' And he immediately said, 'Don't be stupid, of course she will be buried here.' So instead of going to the undertakers, she lay in the Fleming Chapel, where the cadaver tomb is, and after cremation she was buried in the west wall of the cloisters. So I always like to feel that her last years were extremely contented.

I don't see how you can avoid loving this building. But that's an oversimplification. I've got to qualify it by saying I am an extrovert, I love people, I love communicating with people, and the Cathedral offers me a marvellous opportunity to do just that. That's the first thing. The second thing, of course, is that its history for me is not dates, it is entirely people; the Cathedral represents people to me, right from the beginning.

I like to think I invented – this possibly isn't true, but very nearly – the roof tours to the western end. That's my thing. And now, almost automatically, if there's anybody comes in and wants a tour that includes the roof, they instantly ring me up. The Dean passed me on a letter the other day from someone who wanted a tour; automatically, without any hesitation, he just bung the letter at me.

From my very first time here I could see what enormous

potential there was in this, and . . . I sort of worked the whole thing out in my mind, and then when somebody wanted to have a look at the nave roof, I did the tour the way I wanted to do it. Since then it's built up to a point where . . . you must forgive me if I sound a bit brash . . . people go away sort of starry-eyed as it were. The tour that I do is virtually unique, and I hope you'll do it with me sometime.

When I have a receptive group of people who become starry-eyed almost from the beginning, then it's absolutely wonderful. And, believe me, about 80 per cent of them are. But, quite truthfully, it is of secondary importance to me. I do my thing; if they don't like it, that's their fault. Sometimes you have children who have been compelled to come and they're a bit truculent, and sometimes I have to rule the roost about it. If they ignore you and start larking about on Banks' View, which is dangerous, then I have to stop dead and say, 'Shut up,' that sort of thing, because it's tricky up there.

I don't take French up there, the French are awful; everybody in the Cathedral will tell you that. Germans are lovely people. Americans are tolerable and, of course, they are dreadfully, dreadfully friendly. Italians are fine, but nobody speaks their language except me. But French children are the end. I can recall once, there were French children all round the place and one of the vergers had just laid up the Longman's Chantry for early Communion, and two of the girls nipped in there and drank the wine.

I have done two tours in a day, but everyone says don't be so stupid, and I prefer not to do two. At the time, of course, it takes nothing out of you: you're on a high. When I get home my legs hurt, because I've got arthritis in both hips; I shall be due in fairly soon, I suppose, for replacements. But you've got ropes, and I pull myself up on those. By using my hands on the rope, it takes the weight off my hips and I can nip up the stairs fairly easily.

I make up stories. The number of times some elderly lady has come up to me and said, 'Oh, Mr Harvey, you are clever, you know all the history!' And I say, 'I don't, darling, I make it up.'

If you go on a tour of the Cathedral and you know the whole thing by heart, it's so deadly bloody dull – I've heard some of the guides do it. Oh no, I bung the stories in all the time, and I don't care whether they're dead true or slightly true or what; I don't mind as long as they're interesting and amusing.

If the chief verger will allow me to have a key that will double-lock the door, the number three key, I can then say, 'Please lock the place up, ring curfew by all means, and I will be responsible.' Then when I have finished my tour and brought them down, I say, 'Now come into the nave and you can see where you've been.' And there is no other soul in the place and no other light on – it's a quite magical moment, because the nave will be quite dark, except for the fact that the whole of that lovely vault is lit with gold, because the floodlighting is all directed at the clerestory windows, and it comes through. There isn't a single person that's experienced that that's ever been anything other than starry-eyed. They never dreamt that it was going to be like this; they thought they were going to go up to the roof and back again. Very, very often I had the most dewy-eyed sort of thank-yous from people, but it's because I love the place.

BOB HELLOWELL,
PLUMBER AND GLAZIER

I WAS working at a lady's house in the Halifax area and she gave me a newspaper to read while I was sitting out in the garden having a bit of lunch. I noticed this advertisement saying that there was a vacancy in Lincoln for a tenor-cum-carpenter. I happened to be singing baritone at the time and I thought there could be the possibility of a job in the Works Department for me as well, being a plumber, and it turned out to be so, and that's what brought me to Lincoln.

My wife at the time – she died in 1981 – she came from Lincolnshire, she was a Boston girl, but we moved up to Halifax, which is my home ground, and we were always so happy there. But I got involved in a lot of these amateur operatic society dos, and I was doing a bit of the local clubs as well, and it became a bit involved and a bit hectic, so I was glad to move. I saw it as an opportunity to do the singing, which I enjoyed, and also working round the Cathedral area, the environment is so good.

I was stationed around here in the RAF during the war. I was at Swinderby in the first instance, and then at Skellingthorpe with the 50 Squadron. Then I went to Scampton when they formed up 617 Squadron, and I was there during the time of the Dam Raids. I ended up at East Kirkby, and in the course of going out dancing and what-not I met my wife. I was just observing what was going on on the dance floor. I was aware that there was a girl behind me, and I simply turned round on the spur of the moment and asked for a dance. We got along famously right from the start and everything turned out very happily. A lovely lass, oh yes, she was great.

From a distance I had seen the Cathedral, of course, coming down from Scampton, but during the entire war I never actually visited the Cathedral – and there was Dr Slater struggling with his depleted choir, a sort of scratch team. I was very young and naïve at the time, and my interests were more in enjoying myself than any thoughts on visiting cathedrals and such like. But I'd heard what a beautiful place it was, of course, and I can't disagree with that; it really is. I think the whole magnitude, and at the same time the grace, of the structure itself – it's such beautiful proportions compared to lots of other buildings I have seen of a similar ilk, it's so graceful, it's a gem. I do love it.

I am very emotional in some ways, but things of beauty cause me more emotion than anything sad. I can take people losing their babies and things like that quite philosophically, but certain things do make me emotional. There is a certain anthem, 'I Was Glad' by Parry, which I can never resist feeling absolutely . . . it really thrills me, that does. It was offered at Prince Charles's wedding I think, on the entry into St Paul's. There is also Hymn 92 in the English Hymnal, which is a Lenten hymn and has a tune by Thomas Tallis. It's a kind of simple progression of the notation, but it's so beautifully done and so simple in its way that I just heave with emotion, my whole being seems to convulse; it's terrific. The words are something after:

When rising from the bed of death
Sowed by guilt and fear,
I see my saviour face to face
Then how shall I appear?

It goes on like that, beautiful words. The tune was actually developed as a fantasia by Vaughan Williams, and you sometimes hear it as background music on television programmes. It doesn't matter when I hear it – I just thrill at it.

I think I could conscientiously say that I am a religious man now. Before I came to Lincoln, I was a member of the local parish church choir and I attended church, but I didn't know anything. I was pretty dim until I was about 40.

I started learning things by virtue of the fact that I was

working and living around here, and mixing with people that knew more than I did, people who have a more educated outlook on life. It gradually rubs off on you a bit. It's just the fact that they accept you into their confidence and talk to you in a sensible way, and where perhaps you have been lacking in some respects, you gradually learn that there's more to life than you understood there was. I soon developed a friendship with a wonderful chap who was assistant organist here at the time, Clifford Hewis. He's now incarcerated in a home down by the hospital; he's very badly crippled with arthritis, which is a terrible pity. He's suffered that now for fifteen years or so, and he was very proud of his fitness before this came upon him. But he's a wonderful chap, and I struck up a very firm friendship with him, and I miss the friendship because he really was very entertaining, a good sense of humour – in fact, it was a laugh a minute.

I retired from the choir about ten years ago. For one thing, I had lost about a tone and a half at the bottom end of my range, which wasn't a happy thing, and there were things that rather irritated me about the attitudes of certain members of the choir, who seemed to be concerned about radio performances and trips away demonstrating their prowess to others – but I'm probably a bit of an odd bod in that respect. My feelings are that a choir is there for the benefit of the Cathedral worship, and I just got the feeling that there was too much concern about doing performances.

When I was singing in the choir as well as working on the job, there was little else. Apart from my home and family, it was my life. Fortunately, my wife was equally happy to be involved in it. She would attend all the various functions that were on and help with catering and things.

During the time I was in the choir my favourite service was Friday evensong, which was unaccompanied. I really did enjoy that. To me that was the real thing. I used to promise myself that when I retired from the choir, I would attend Friday evensong, but, I don't know, I just seem to keep so well occupied. I'm semi-retired now – I was 65 in January – and I spend just two days a week working on the Cathedral, but I don't seem to have time to do all the things I want to do.

JOHN HURD, CONSERVATOR

MY first sight of the Cathedral was when I was about 10 and I came up with my father. What he was doing here I don't know – he was a salesman, seeing a client I guess – and he left me in the Cathedral for the morning. There is a piece of graffiti in there of a ship. A boy got locked in the Cathedral one night way back, 1760s, and he was frightened and took a candle from the altar, and hid himself in a corner and scratched an outline of his father's ship on one of the wood panels. That was a very early prime mover in my life. I was very impressed by that and I just sat in this little niche and looked at this guy's ship. I remember that very clearly. What a wonderful place; I mean, as a child, it was just so huge.

After I moved up to Lincolnshire, I came and looked at that ship again. I had never imagined that I would work here strangely enough, but I am very happy to work here; what an extraordinary place.

I started work helping to restore the Christopher Wren library. It was painted apple green, and under five layers of various vile colours of paint was Wren's original decorative scheme, white and black Italian marbling and *trompe-l'œil* panels and so forth. I came to do some of the work taking off the green paint, and some of the repainting and gilding, which is a skill I learnt in my cabinet-making days.

The original Wren craftsmen had left behind them little visual jokes everywhere – in the marbling there would be a profile of a face, or a name written. We found all sorts of little visual jokes as we scraped away, bottoms, fingers in noses, various rude jokes.

And I guess they were all the naughtier for it being a place of worship.

What happened was very peculiar. I worked there alone – hundreds of hours I spent in that library working alone – and as I worked I got a definite sense of craftsmanship down the ages, I got a shot of 1676. And sometimes while I was gilding I used to feel as if there were twenty or thirty very critical cantankerous old buggers standing behind me looking at my work. It was a very strange experience, but a lovely experience. They were kind of approving, but I think they felt that I should have served a seventeen-year apprenticeship before I set to gilding.

If you want to do marbling such as in the Wren library, you can't do it in the way they did it unless you have got the same brushes. A nylon one just doesn't do it. You can no longer buy badger-hair softeners, hog's-hair floggers, squirrel-hair fitches and whips; they don't exist any more; quite rightly so, cruel to animals to make them. But you need that same sense of history and you just can't express it properly unless you are using the tools that were originally used. So we did the Wren library using original tools, and there is something remarkably fine about using original tools. I have got quite a collection. They are quite valuable, but they are more valuable to me than cash. My badger-hair softener, which is a paintbrush only three inches wide, cost me £120, but it will last me my lifetime if it's looked after, and it will go on to last someone else theirs, I'm sure.

At the moment I am examining every door and screen; in fact, every piece of woodwork in the Cathedral. The first project is to get all the doors cleaned and restored and provenanced, and as no one has ever done the doors, no one really knows how old they are. I have had many pleasant days staring at doors, and I am surprised to find that they go right back to the beginning of the Cathedral. The earliest door appears to be mid-thirteenth century, which is the Russell Chantry door. The screens in the transepts are also of that date, 1275, I should think. Fascinating stuff, because the screen bases have got break fronts to allow for pillars. Of course, they hadn't invented the mitre or anything to make a moulding, so they carved these things out of solid oak, and they are extraordinary, they really are.

I've spent fourteen days on the great West Door; it's a kind of puny contribution when faced with the whole, but by the same token there is a continuity of craft going back a thousand years of which you are a link. That is a wonderful thing, quite humbling. Those doors have been there for hundreds of years and will be there for hundreds of years longer; it is quite belittling in a sense.

There is something distinctive about medieval wood. I guess it is the technology with which it is made: the wood has never been forced to do anything it doesn't want to, everything is built according to the very nature of the wood. To start with, a twelfth-century door is made with riven planks rather than sawn planks, which means that one side of the plank is thicker than the other because a wedge of tree adds down, so each plank goes from the sap to the heart, and it is always narrower at the heart and wider at the sap. I like that very much and am very sorry that it is not done like that today. Cut a piece of wood with a saw and you get an altogether different thing – you only have to look at the wood in the Cathedral to see what I mean.

My first job was with a cabinet-maker who was restoring medieval furniture, and it never satisfied me. If you had a very wormy carving or moulding on a piece of medieval furniture, you would hack it out and put in new wood and make good, and I always thought that was a shame in a way. Besides, when you are dealing with fourteenth-century oak, like St Hugh's Choir, it is hardly appropriate. So I started doing it another way, impregnating wood with waxes and polyethylene glycols and so on to see if there was a way of making wood strong. No one in this country treats medieval wood in that way, although they do it with stone, bronze, statuary, archive books and textiles.

People are very interested in watching conservators at work. They always ask what you're doing, and I say, 'Trying to concentrate.' But people want to talk to you and find out more. I think they are looking for little insider bits of history that the ordinary tour guide wouldn't give you perhaps. A lot of people say, 'Were

I younger, I would go into this field. How lucky you are.' I love talking to people, but it is hard when you are twenty feet up a ladder. And they do insist. I have even had people shaking the ladder and saying, 'Excuse me,' which is quite hairy!

I hope to work in other cathedrals. Recently I was approached by the Cathedrals Advisory Council, who were telling me there are wood projects in Canterbury, Hereford and Durham in particular, of a very urgent nature.

But I shall always look upon Lincoln as being the seed of it all, for sure. It is a wonderful cathedral, isn't it? I have been to many, many cathedrals in Germany, Spain and France, and all over England, and they have each got their wonders, but all in all none of them elevates my spirits as much as Lincoln does. When you walk in through the West Door and you gaze up at that incredible vaulting, it is marvellous.

I get a rather horrifying sense of what the Church has done over the last thousand years. It was built as a fortress more or less. The Norman part, Remegius's bit, was a fortified church, and one has to look back over 1,000 years of extraordinary power and possible abuse. But I think the fact that it has survived, and survived as it is today, is quite remarkable and wonderful, and I do feel that continuity.

I dream of the Cathedral all the time. I have had dreams about Cromwell's hordes camping in there and tying their horses to the pillars and lighting fires in the nave and pissing up the walls, and I've dreamed of other periods in history as well. I do tend to have historic dreams.

THE VERY REVEREND BRANDON JACKSON, DEAN*

I WAS brought up in Cheshire, the Manchester end of Cheshire rather than the Liverpool end. I'm one of seven children. I suppose you'd say we were fairly straightforward working class, and my generation was the first generation off to university. My father was extremely intelligent, but had not had a formal education and he suffered as a result, and he was determined that his boys and girls would go on to university. We did go on to university, and we're eternally grateful to him.

In 1946, when I was a 12-year-old, the whole direction of our family life changed course. It was the death of my great-grandmother, who had lived with us and was a sort of quasi-mother really. She was a greatly loved figure in the family, and because of her death we went to church – you go to church on the Sunday after a funeral; that was the custom then in that part of England. We'd no intentions of going again, but, fortunately, the church was vitally alive there. There was a superb young curate, who had a great gift of personal evangelism, and he talked to my father, and my father said on the way out of church, 'You will see us next Sunday.' We all groaned and when we got home, we had a sort of private council of war with my mother, and she said, 'Don't worry, your father'll never keep this lot up!' But we went the following Sunday and he said, 'You'll see us

*I spoke with Brandon Jackson in Bradford one month after the official announcement of his appointment as Dean of Lincoln, and one month before he was due to move there.

next week,' and, really, we began to enjoy it. We were going to Matins and the 1662 prayer book was a foreign language to us, but we learned all the canticles and the psalms, the sermons were always worth listening to, and we came to love it. There is no doubt that the faith that came to my father, through conversion, meant that my mother got a better husband and we got a better father, and one by one we simply came to the faith.

My conversion was gradual. I can only say that I went into the tunnel period of May 1946, when great-grandmother died, to May 1947 not being a Christian and came out of it converted. I knew then that I was a Christian. There were certain things happening in my life that made me realize. For instance, I'd stopped cheating at school in exams, I tried to stop swearing and doing all the snotty, dirty little things that boys do at that age. Not that I became a goody-goody; I still boxed, and I went on to box for the school and was lightweight champion; I played cricket and rugby for the school, and so on, so I didn't become prissy – I was a bit of a wild young fellow. But there was a distinct change in my life, and my mates at school noticed it.

I went up to university to read law, because I did intend being a lawyer. It was during my undergraduate days I began to realize I had to take religion seriously, especially when my tutor wrote a reference for me, saying, 'I think his first love is not the law.' I asked him what he meant, and he said, 'Well, one day you will be ordained. My conviction is that one day you will find your calling, and your vocation is in the Church rather than the law.' Things like that were a bit of a surprise to me, because I didn't realize that people were aware of the strength of the convictions that were within me.

I went to talk to the rector at my church, and he said, 'I think what the good Lord is saying is, "Stop running away." You are really putting off what God is saying to you.' That was confirmed to me at a Selection Board, and I went on to read theology at Oxford and then was ordained.

There are people who say they've had revelations and all sorts of fantastic, dramatic things. Nothing like that ever seems to happen to me. Every decision I have made, not least this Lincoln decision, there's never been anything sensational, but a growing conviction that this is what I must be doing.

Lincoln came into my life about three days before Christmas. It was not only a surprise, I was, to be honest, quite angry with God. I knew that the time had come for me to leave Bradford. I'd felt this for about eighteen months – I'd finished the job I perceived God had called me to do at Bradford, therefore, let's move on to something else. I didn't know what it would be, but I had made it very plain to the powers that be that I would never contemplate doing another cathedral after Bradford. I had found the experience very painful; I felt I was not a natural cathedral type of person. The pageantry and the inevitable pomp, all the dignity and honour and so forth that goes on, and the comparative remoteness from the people as distinct from parish church ministry, were things that I have always found difficult to come to terms with. I don't like to be distanced from the people. To go from a cosy parish church cathedral to one as magnificent, splendid and enormous as Lincoln, was something that I did not relish.

I didn't even know that my good friend Oliver was retiring. I simply got a letter from No. 10 Downing Street, saying, '. . . My dear Provost, you will know that the Very Reverend the Honourable Oliver Twisleton-Wykeham-Fiennes is retiring from the Deanery of Lincoln this next January, and I would like to nominate your name to the Queen to take his place.' I wrote immediately saying what I've just said to you . . . I never contemplated doing another cathedral again, nevertheless if you require that I consider this, I will pray hard about it, I'll think hard, I'll consult and make a decision and write to you again. The Prime Minister's Appointments Secretary, Robin Catford, got on the phone to me and said, 'The Prime Minister has received your letter and I want you to know she's taking a personal interest in this appointment. She is from Grantham, which is within the Diocese of Lincoln, and so this is her cathedral.'

I was in Lincoln yesterday and it was most impressive. To come up the A46 and see this magnificent pile on the hill was really breathtaking . . . but going there to have a wander round after I received the letter – my first time in Lincoln – it didn't thrill me. It was damp and cold; it was a dreadful day. My old car was giving me an awful lot of trouble – the gasket had gone and water was getting into the engine, and we did have a bit of trouble getting there. I put my nose into the Chapter House and that smelled musty. I went into the Refectory and there were a couple of young girls behind the counter quarrelling with one another, and one was more concerned with her relationship with the other girl than with me. We looked around and, to be honest, I didn't think I'd be going. It's only yesterday that it fair took my breath away. Yesterday, coming up from the south, that really did it. I was most moved by it because it so dominates the skyline. It was a lovely sunny morning and seeing the Cathedral, with such beautiful lines, so slender and elegant, and tall and magnificent – massive but not with the bulk of Durham – there's an eloquence there that was most moving yesterday. It made me realize what special people those who built that cathedral must have been, people with enormous commitment and vision of God.

Bradford's cathedral is squat and solid and dependable, like Yorkshire folk. It isn't beautiful in the sense that Lincoln is, but then Bradford is not a place of beauty and the people do not have an eye for beauty: this is a place of wool mills and brass bands. So unconscious of beauty are they, that the most magnificent medieval building they have, and almost the only one that they preserved – their cathedral – they allowed to be hidden by building the Post Office in front of it so they can't even see it. Having made their river into a sort of open sewer, they then covered that over to keep themselves healthy. When people do that, they cannot have a sense of the beauty and order in creation. And that's the kind of people they are. I love them and I've really enjoyed working here, but there are still people saying, 'Have we got a cathedral in Bradford?' No one can ever say that in Lincoln.

Finally, what did it, what made me decide to take on the job, was on 8 January, which is the first Sunday after the Epiphany, I was preaching a sermon, the title and subject of which had been chosen by the Canon Precentor. And I said, 'Here we are at the beginning of the year. Pray God He'll give you a word from Heaven about where you're to go and what you're to be doing about your Father's business this year . . .' and there in my own stall in Bradford, having preached a sermon to others, I realized God was preaching it at me or had got me to preach it at myself. I knew then that I had to go. Sitting up in bed that evening I said, 'Mary, what do you think?' And she said, 'It's so obvious that sermon was right for you', and that was that. I was happily convinced that this constituted the call of God. And we are excited about going.

I'm obviously going to be a different Dean. Oliver is an Old Etonian and from one of the oldest and finest families of the realm. He said in a television programme they made on his retirement, *The Dean's Farewell*, that when King John signed Magna Carta at Runnymede, one of his ancestors was a witness to the King's signature. If one of my ancestors was there, he'd have been one of his serfs. And therefore there's bound to be a difference.

I knew that it would be very hard to disengage from Bradford, to which I have given everything I had; all that I am I've given to Bradford. Also, I'm a hoarder. Mary isn't, Mary gets rid of things, but I've hoarded all sorts of things, and it's going to be very painful sorting out my garage and my workbench and all my wood. I can't take lumps of wood down there, but I like my wood . . . I want to make things out of it. It's pieces of seasoned oak, which is valuable wood; if you went to a timber yard to buy it, it would be expensive. But what do I do with it? They'll think I'm mad taking loads of wood there.

At the moment we've nowhere to live. Oliver described the Deanery as being medieval open plan and totally inappropriate; it's like a big baronial mansion; massive, irregular-shaped rooms. He's right, it isn't suitable for a deanery. You can't keep warm in the place. When Mary said to Juliet, 'What do you do?', she said, 'We just put more woollies on!' Well, Oliver was brought up in a castle, so he's probably accustomed to living in a great big baronial mansion with enormous rooms, but we would never keep warm there. I don't want to have anything posh and slick, but we need a comfortable base from which to operate.

I'm very humbled to think I'm going to such a lovely place, very excited about it. I've had hundreds of people kindly writing to me, literally hundreds saying 'Congratulations, we're so glad you're going.' To everyone, I've said, 'Please pray for us. I know that I can do nothing in my own strength, but with God all things are possible.'

It sheer takes my breath away to think I'm going to that magnificent place, and I'll feel very puny and small in it. I think that's one of the great things about a building like that: it humbles you. If I feel so puny and small in a building like that, how much more insignificant am I in the very presence of the Living God? Because, as Solomon said of his temple, that was as nothing compared with the greatness of God.

BEN KENDAL, CHORISTER

I AM 12½, and have been in the choir for three years. One Saturday afternoon Mum said would I like to go in for the Lincoln Cathedral choir, it was advertised in the paper. I went into the Cathedral school and sang a piece of music. I chose 'Lead Me Lord'. I did all right. I was very nervous, my stomach felt a bit . . . kept rumbling. My voice is not excellent, not bad, just in between.

Most of us aren't angels or anything, we all mess around on the odd occasion. Maybe one or two mess around a lot. David Pace likes laughing a lot, and if anyone does anything that is funny, he just starts laughing. A lot of people seem to be worshipping in the Cathedral, so it makes you feel kind of holier. But sermons are a bit . . . no one likes them. They are really boring. Throughout the fifteen minutes we are all fooling around generally.

We have a blue robe, a ruff and surplice, which is the white thing over the cassock. When you are in your robes all the tourists notice you and they start taking photographs and all things like that. I don't really mind; it's all right. A good feeling.

We sing at the St Hugh's Choir, which is this quite big kind of area, and we go on tours sometimes. We have been going out to other churches and singing. There are about seven or eight hymns that I specially like. I like 'Jerusalem', that's really all right.

At Lincoln the organ is nice because it is so loud. In my old choir it sounded different because it was a lot quieter. This choir feels really good and it is really nice to be in it.

There are four people in the choir who wear black robes and are called coat boys, who are chosen every year to be in charge. I will be one of those. It is quite a good feeling, I was really pleased. We won't be making any new rules. Sometimes the coat boys used to get a bit unpopular because if we were out of line or had our hands in our pockets we got told off by them, things like that. But we have made a plan that we are not going to be bossy or anything.

Philip Millward is very musical. He plays the piano, cello and other musical instruments, and he has got perfect pitch. He just knows so much about music. His father's in the choir. Ian South has got a very nice voice. He usually does all the hard pieces because he is the only one who can cope with it. He is a coat boy. David Page is very good at music and has just about got perfect pitch. He likes singing a lot. He is the smallest boy in the choir – he's very small – but he is really nice when you get used to him, and always being happy and never moaning. Philip Davies is a coat boy and nice, and Midge Gold is a coat boy. Tristram Hillier is very bright, he's going to Harrow. James Bradley is doing well. He is going to become a good singer when he grows up. Matthew Birch is doing well. He joined the same time as me and has become a very good singer. He's always laughing and pulling funny faces so his eyes go all funny and that. He is really nice to know. He can make himself go really, really deep red. He's ever so funny.

Philip Millward is called Milly; Ian South is called Southy or Ian; Michael John Gold is called Midge; David Page is called Tiddles because he is so small; Philip Davies is just Davies or Philip; Tristram is Trist; James Bradley is Bradley; my nickname is Bendal. The men don't have nicknames – we daren't.

Sam Wilson's voice broke about a year ago. He was due to go on for another year, but he had to leave. It was pretty sad because he was a really nice person in the choir and always funny and never bossing you around, and he was a really good singer, but he just went because his voice broke.

I'll be very sad when my voice breaks. Very. It is really good fun, and there are lots of brilliant things that you can do in the choir, like going abroad to France and Germany, and there are lots of friends in the choir. This school is good because you only have two exams a year overall. It is called Lincoln Cathedral School. All the choir is there. I like school at the moment, but when we get to our next school, then it is going to be hard work, so it is all going to change.

I will probably carry on in the school choir. I haven't really chosen yet, maybe Uppingham, or Sedbergh. When I grow up I would like to be a doctor, but I am not really sure what I will become.

JOHN LARSON,
VICTORIA AND ALBERT MUSEUM

MY specialist field is sculpture conservation, and that covers an enormous range of objects – everything from Indian, Chinese, Japanese, to all sorts of European sculptures. Over the years, because we're one of the few places in the world that specialize in sculpture conservation, I've got very much involved with work for the National Trust, country houses, churches, cathedrals, giving them advice on how they should care for things.

I've been involved with most of the major cathedral sculpture projects in this country, but we've withdrawn from those, because, both personally and from the point of view of the museum, we were very unhappy about what was being done there. We didn't think the approach was right. I feel the Dean and Chapter of Lincoln have been good. They seem to have given a lot of thought to the problem, which is quite at variance with the way other cathedrals approached it. And I think that as a result of that, finally what will be done there will be that much more successful.

I was involved in a television programme about the problems of pollution and acid rain on stone and how it affected our most valuable buildings. I was then approached directly by Lincoln asking me if I would be interested in being involved with the conservation of the Romanesque Frieze. I was very concerned about the condition of the Frieze because I'd been asked to inspect it by the Cathedral's Advisory Committee about twelve years ago, and really nothing much had happened about it for some years.

The Romanesque Frieze is a fairly unified decorative skin,

twelfth-century, running right across the façade of the West Front of Lincoln Cathedral as a series of sculptured reliefs, something like four feet tall, comprising about twenty to twenty-two reliefs, each of which has an individual scene or panel. It's a very important sculpture for this country – it's extraordinarily important – because we have so little comparable material; most of it has been destroyed.

The condition of the sculpture is variable. Some of it is in very bad condition and some of it's amazingly good. Considering its age, some of the sculpture is remarkably crisp. The greatest damage to the stone is where rainwater has run over the surface. Those areas where the sills above the sculpture have deteriorated, water has then poured over the surface of the sculpture, mixing with the pollutant on the outside, and produced acids that literally eat away the stone. In those areas that are protected, you have incredible detail still left, entrapped in a thick layer of black pollutant, so, ironically, in some ways pollution has saved some of it.

At the moment commercial conservators are being used to do the cleaning and the conservation, but the idea is that Lincoln should eventually have its own people permanently based there, who will deal with these problems. If you take the whole Cathedral, you have maybe 10,000 pieces of sculpture, a vast number of bits and pieces of sculpture, a lot of which are superb in quality. So you're talking about a very long project, which is equivalent to someone working in a museum. I think at the moment the real problem is to get on and decide what we're going to do with the Frieze. That is going to be in itself an enormous task, and it's going to be very expensive, and it's going to take a lot of time.

You can't wrap it up in cotton-wool. This is the great dilemma for everyone. You cannot build museums fast enough and big enough to hold everything that we have outdoors at present; it would just be impossible. Partly, you accept a degree of decline or loss in the objects. You also try to carry out treatments that forestall that decline, because we have treatments, chemical phosphates, we can apply that will hold things for two or three decades, maybe, in their present form. But we don't have a total preservative.

Pollution and its association with the deterioration of stone is well documented. There are thousands of papers from the late nineteenth century on how industrial pollution is affecting the stone, and Lincoln themselves were horrified when they found old photographs of some of the sculptures that showed enormous losses: literally half of some carved figures had disappeared within fifty or seventy years, showing extraordinary attrition.

The Department of the Environment have a weather station at Lincoln and they're monitoring the level of pollution. They say that the sulphur dioxide level, which is the most researched aspect of pollution damage on stone, is, in fact, much lower than it was in the Sixties and Seventies. But we have added complications now that it's not just the sulphur dioxide that causes troubles: there's CO_2 and nitrous oxides, which are combining with the sulphur dioxide to produce a very complex pollution cocktail. A lot of people are fearful that that is causing as much damage as previously, if not more. You also have the enormous expansion of pollution fumes from cars, which in Lincoln, as everywhere else, has grown phenomenally in the last ten or twenty years. And weathering patterns have changed, so that pollution moves in vast belts. In fact, our pollution is affecting Scandinavian areas several hundreds of miles away: so you're dealing with something that is much more global. Therefore whether there is a brickworks or power station up the road is no longer of such significance – pollution is a much more complicated thing.

You can't be optimistic. It's not that you're dealing just with practical problems; you're dealing with huge emotional problems. People are very much against taking the sculpture off the West Front and putting it indoors, even though that is obviously the safest solution: you can guarantee if it goes indoors it will last for several hundred years more. But people say, 'But it's only significance is if it stays on the West Front. If you put it indoors, it's lost it's meaning.' Then you have to argue with people and say, 'Well, do you want the sculpture or don't you?' They may feel its significance is up there, but if that means the next generation won't see it, aren't they being selfish, and wouldn't it be better to leave it in a museum where, say, in 500 years' time people may have wonderful scientific methods of preserving it and may be able to put it back up again? Maybe the world will be so wonderfully pure by then that we will be able to put anything outdoors.

My view is that you must do what you can at the time. What we have to do is set up an accurate system of recording deterioration so that we can look at a piece of sculpture in two, three or five years' time and say, 'No, we can't leave it up there because in X years' time we will have lost so much that we are just allowing it to fall to pieces.' Unfortunately, we haven't done that so far, and my job now is to make sure this will be done, so that when we discuss whether something's falling to pieces or not, we are talking about accurate data.

You see, nowadays we look at sculpture under a microscope, so our perception of what is there is that much more refined, the stone is magnified anything up to 200 times. Where once upon a time people looked at a piece of sculpture and said, 'The nose has fallen off,' or 'An ear has dropped off,' we now see infinitely more detail. I have noticed since the one panel was cleaned last year that quite a lot of damage has been done. Now the majority of people wouldn't even notice, but because we have worked on it microscopically, we can see that quite a lot has gone, and as far as we're concerned, it's quite a significant amount.

GORDON LAUDER, DOMUS SUPERVISOR

MY oldest son was in the Cubs and he said, 'Isn't it time you came to church for the church parade, Dad?' So I started going and I got really involved, and I've become a server and a sacristan of the church and all sorts.

We've got six children and we always said that when the last one left school we'd move up into this area – because my mother comes from Lincolnshire, you see – and when the youngest one left school, we did. Oh yes, crumbs, I love living up here. I live out at Swinderby, gorgeous little village, about six miles south of Lincoln. We've got quite a big garden and it's absolutely lovely. Smashing people, Lincolnshire people. I find them very, very nice, very friendly people.

The wife's quite happy about it. It was as much her decision as mine to move. I daren't have done it without her. I do as I'm told, like all good husbands.

I've always been a maintenance fitter, actually. I got my indentures as a mechanical engineer and most of my life I was working for a little family firm at Ashtead in Surrey.

I've got the lovely title here of Domus Supervisor. What that means is what nobody else wants to do, I do! I am the engineer as well. You've got stonemasons and joiners, and there's brickies and plumbers, but everything else is done by me. Whatever needs to be done on the bells and the clock itself, we maintain, though that doesn't take much maintaining – it's a lovely machine. We do all the metal work, the locks, we do all the security of the place, the fire and alarm system – we have to keep our eyes on that. We hope we never have to do that sort of thing, but we've got pumps and various things.

Of course, it's much more than a job. It is the most gorgeous building to work in, it really is. I really love it: it's a funny word isn't it, but yes I think I do – definitely do, in fact. It's got some marvellous atmospheres at different times of the day. First thing in the morning it's got a fabulous atmosphere, you could cut it with a knife; you know, that sort of atmosphere. Well, it's as though there is a presence, I suppose is the way to say it. I'm not deeply religious in that sense, but there's definitely a presence in there. I don't really know how to say it. It's so dead still, and yet it's not still, if you know what I mean; it's a fabulous feeling.

And then it's entirely different when you get it full of people. It's just like a railway station. I don't say the presence goes, but it's entirely different. Then when you get a service on, you get another different feeling again.

Then there are different seasons. I've heard it referred to as the biggest refrigerator in the country! It could be, it could well be. Certainly it gets very, very cold. It's due to the stone floors, I think. It seems to come up your legs: your feet get cold first and it gradually works its way up.

Working on the Cathedral you get a different attitude to your work. Even the youngsters, our young masons and apprentices, they've got it already. I don't mean you make a special effort – your work's your work, isn't it? – but you won't have anybody saying anything about the place, not against it anyway. It's a funny attitude.

I quite often look at other cathedrals. There's not another one to touch this one. They've all got their things, of course, their little bits and pieces, but this one seems to be complete in itself. The style in which it is built, I think that is perhaps what does it.

I always have a tour every morning, when I wander around with a black bag in my hand picking up bits of rubbish and what have you, and I'll go to the mason foreman and have a natter about what needs doing or I'll talk to the joiners or whoever.

I see a lot of decay. It seems to have come on at a rate lately. Since I've been here some of these little carved heads on the West End seem to have deteriorated quite badly. Not the building; the building's quite safe enough, don't get me wrong. It's just these little carvings, they're losing their sharpness it seems to me.

There are quite a lot of places where we don't take the public. We daren't. They'd go over the side. Up in the inside of these west towers you can go straight over the side. Of course, knowing what people are like, we have them all boarded up. There are one or two secret places; there's one up on the top windows that was used as a treasury at one time. The only way you can get to it is by going up on the windowsills and then getting a ladder through the window and walking along through a doorway. And you've got little windows looking down on the West Door, which we think were guardrooms, because in the days of King Stephen the Cathedral was used as a castle.

You've got to be very careful with the public, they're terrible people really. It's a funny thing to say, but they can cause an awful lot of damage. Just walking. Next time you go in there, you look up the south aisle in the nave – there's a groove where people have walked straight up the centre. All that stone will have to be replaced eventually. They leave beer cans under altars and things like that. Never full ones though, that's the trouble; you wouldn't mind if they left a few full ones! We don't have a tremendous chewing-gum problem like they do at York, thank goodness: they reckon a bucketful every three months or something.

We don't really have much trouble in Lincoln; it's very lucky really. You occasionally get a little bit of graffiti appear somewhere, which you have to get off pretty smart. You get children smoking; they get up there at night and you find matchsticks and bits of burnt paper. Those doors will take an awful lot of lighting up to burn, but still it's a worry.

The Works Department has got a lot bigger since I've been here. They've really taken a lot on and they're beginning to get on and do big jobs. We didn't have the staff before, so you just couldn't do it. I think it's marvellous. It's a young department. We've got only two who are sort of 40 and over; the rest of them are in their early twenties, and we've recently got a mason apprentice, a joiner apprentice, plumber apprentice and an electrician apprentice, so the future is assured with this young department; it's fantastic.

I'm the ancient member of the department. I'm called 'Uncle', and I call for my 'nephews' if I want anything lifted – I'm told to just move over while something's being lifted.

THE VENERABLE CHRISTOPHER LAURENCE, ARCHDEACON

I HAVE roots here. My father was a parson here, my grandfather was a parson here, and my great-grandfather was a parson here; so that goes back a bit.

I hug my Jewish background rather. My great-great-great-grandfather was a merchant in Venice. He came over in 1780 and set up a stockbroker firm, which is still going. Then his wife, who was a Sebag-Montefiore, converted, and each of their ten children converted and became clergymen – it was quite an extraordinary thing. Then all the sons of that generation became clergymen too, and amongst them was my great-grandfather. He was a very good clergyman, and when he came to a little village in Lincolnshire called Welsby, he bought the patronage of the living and settled down very happily.

I have lived in sight of the Cathedral from childhood onwards. We lived in a little village nineteen miles east of here, and Lincoln Cathedral hangs on the horizon all the way round for dozens of miles, so a great deal of my life has been spent in sight of this building. It's quite a thought.

In those days the Cathedral had rather a neglected kind of feel to it. There weren't many people visiting it and when you walked around, it was rather impersonal and so it didn't excite me particularly, romantically, as a child.

In large parts of Lincolnshire, while acknowledging it is an essential part of Lincolnshire, there is a strong antipathy to the Cathedral, because it is so dominant. There is a sort of antipathy towards everything it stands for, a strange kind of love–hate relationship, which you could have a lovely time explaining in psychological terms, and I come from that in a sense. Here am I saying that I have lived most of my life in sight of the Cathedral, and have enjoyed this thing on the horizon known as 'The Cathedral', which was the place of hope the bombers aimed for when they were trying to get back to their Lincolnshire base, and when they saw the Cathedral they knew they had got home; and I used to see them hobbling back in 1943 all shot up. And so there is all the symbolic meaning that has become woven into the Cathedral. And yet, knowing all that, still having this resistance to it, it's a strange kind of paradox.

It's distracting to have such a magnificent building. That's why I buck at it. My own frame of worship is I am a people person; I like the kind of worship that is people orientated, and the form of worship a cathedral has is opposite to the kind I naturally gravitate towards. My own belief is that the Christian Church is about learning in Christ to love one another, in other words, to be a community. Cathedral worship is about transcendence; the music is intellectual, it belittles the human person. A little girl said to me after she came out of the service just last Sunday, 'I could see it,' she said, 'but it couldn't see me', and that's what's at fault, I think, with cathedral worship.

But it's a gorgeous distraction. Sometimes the music sends shivers up my spine when it really takes off. There is also the romantic sense about it, it stands there so beautifully. I travel in very frequently at night from all kinds of distances, and to see that place just hanging there, floodlit, representing home and so much more, is always moving. For me it has that sense of romanticism, it symbolizes something to do with place, home, identity.

It is a glorious place when the sun is shining in in the morning, or you're walking through it in the dark when there is just the floodlighting shining in from outside, which is a lovely golden colour. It is a most inspiring place. It is seductive, and I know that I am now in the process of being seduced by the damn place. I am a kind of reluctant victim, but I know I am being seduced.

Having been brought up in a Christian school, and living in a country area where the Church and community were integrated, going into the army on National Service helped me to see what a very peripheral thing the Church and Christianity are in a wider context. I was a subaltern in the Lincolnshire Regiment at a time when it had just come out of Palestine, this is 1948. The regiment had had a very bad time because they were being shot at by both Arab and Israeli, and when they came into Egypt, which is when I joined them, they were very sore, and my first impression was the low value on human life if it happened not to be British. Our treatment of the Egyptians was very often quite appalling; it was quite a sharp experience. I actually saw torture and all kinds of things in the army, and I realized the need for Christianity through seeing it perceived as peripheral. And it was that, I think, that convinced me of my own identity within the Church, and it was the natural thing to wish to serve it professionally. That was the dawning of my vocation.

I had a diary, and I noted in my diary that was the first time I began to think seriously about God. Up to then I had been in a Christian milieu where you just went along in quite a conventional way of life in the Christian faith. So I offered myself for ordination, and went straight to Cambridge after coming out of the army. There was a sense, yes, here is a calling, this is what I was meant for, so I must do it.

An archdeacon is responsible for an area of the diocese, an episcopal area. He is concerned with what I call the temporalities, what you might call the practical side: the parsonages, the pay, the church buildings, the maintenance, the gutters, all that sort of thing. And I have Lindsey, which is quite the best part of Lincolnshire to be wandering about in. It's the east of Lincolnshire, from the Humber down to the Fens and most of the Wolds; lovely, lovely, great big rolling wolds. As you travel over them you suddenly see in the heart of these wolds this enormous great spire shooting up, and you find this magnificent eighteenth-century town of Louth.

We have something like 200 medieval buildings to look after, and each building has two church wardens to look after it, ordinary people who have taken on the job. They have huge problems, because it costs enormous sums of money to maintain these buildings, funded solely by voluntary funds. Imagine the problem, for example, of a village of only 120 souls that has a beautiful medieval church that needs £30,000 to be spent on its tower. They have to find the money, they have to see what kind of grants might be available, and they have to see how much money they can raise locally, and sometimes, incredibly, they find the money. I can be helpful in this respect, where funds can be found, or supporting applications for grants, and so on.

Legally speaking, they can't do anything to one of these churches without an archdeacon's certificate, called a 'faculty'. I set up an advisory committee so that whatever work is done has some kind of assurance that it will be of reasonable quality.

One of the problems about archdeacons' lives is that we are the committee men of the diocese – I belong to thirty-nine committees. So the archdeacon's job is very much confined by the amount of committees he has to attend, but in between those times, he needs to be travelling around looking at churches and vicarages, and finding out what's going on. I see it as part of my job to know every parish. In a way it is quite unspiritual, which is good for my soul, I think.

One of my other duties is to attend Chapter meetings in the Cathedral. The Dean and Chapter meet fortnightly. It's a very formal procedure: we sit round a table and we begin with formal prayer, and we go right through from ten o'clock until lunch time.

I would say that the Chapter don't get on in any way that people normally get on because we meet only in role, we barely ever meet in person. I was horrified when I first came and at Chapter meetings we addressed each other as Mr Dean and Mr Precentor, Mr Subdean and Mr Chancellor. There are only five of us, after all, sitting round a table. I now see how necessary it is that we do meet in role, although I am sorry that we don't actually meet very often in person.

In fact, we are quite ordinary human beings. We would probably be quite nice to each other if we weren't in that particular kind of relationship. But I guess we all think we know how something should be done, and, of course, it's never how the other chap thinks it should be done, in terms of priorities, in terms of expenditure, in terms of liturgy, and those are contentious issues in any terms.

The relationship between the Dean and the Precentor is a theme around which one could hang a whole book. One theme could be the personal level: here are two men of entirely different outlook and background, locked together over twenty years, each of them appearing to be in antipathy to what the other one stands for in terms of liturgy and the understanding of Christianity itself. And then there is the Cathedral itself: what is the Cathedral about, this building that is actually holding together these two polarities within itself, and what does that do for it? The whole development of Christian understanding in our own time could all be focused on that relationship.

I think it has forced the Precentor into a deep loneliness, because there is nobody in the Chapter who is in sympathy with his ideals for liturgy, for the dignity of the Church as he sees it, and so on. He very much represents, to me at any rate, eighteenth-century ideals. He's very well read, he's a very learned man, he is very courteous, he is offended by vulgarity and the kind of camaraderie and chumminess that go with Christianity today. All his ideals have been challenged and swept aside by the impatient members of the Chapter who are for modernity and for vernacular language, for dispensing with Latin, and making the place open to one and all, having people coming in and dancing in the aisles; all that sort of thing is a shock to his system.

Just occasionally there are times when he produces a very sensible suggestion and the Chapter do take it up gratefully. It isn't an unmitigated disaster for him or the Chapter. The Chapter do try, I think, very hard indeed to honour him as a person, and to be friendly with him, but what's going on and why the Chapter are opposed to him are to do with very deep principles.

But you imagine being opposed, alone, against four others,

when you know that your view will be overlooked at each turn of events for twenty years, and what that must do to you.

The Dean himself has suffered for twenty years an attitude to which he is wholly opposed. He is somebody who wants to open the Church to all people; being an aristocrat, he is very much for the common man. It has been said that if you want to be married in the Cathedral, the one way in which you can be sure that your application will fail is if you say that you are highly connected, whereas if you are anything else, then he will welcome you. So he stands for Christianity for all people; he doesn't like preciousness in music, he doesn't like to hear Latin being sung because nobody understands it.

I think that any sense of humour about the Precentor, or indeed the Dean and Chapter, has probably long since evaded him because it has been such a very, very painful relationship, and your novel could end with the defeat of the Dean, this battle which has gone on for twenty years, and finally the Dean retires and the Precentor stays on for another ten or fifteen years.

The Dean is indeed leaving; he's retiring. The Precentor will go on until he dies. It is a fascinating character study. Here is this very gentle, very polite man, who will never speak unless he is being spoken to, would never intrude upon a conversation, you always have to draw him in, who will never force himself. And yet he has a will of iron. In the end this mild, quiet, well-mannered man has, you could say, ousted the Dean and hung on triumphantly. Depends how you write your novel.

I think you could say that the Precentor has won. If he had gone, we might have had Oliver as Dean for a little bit longer. Mind you, I think that Oliver is right in many ways to leave now, for his own sake, and also after twenty years, it's a good thing to have a new dean. But he has done a superb job, has Oliver, and it has cost him a great deal to do it. In personal costs I think it has torn him up because it has brought him such frustration. He sees what should be done, he sees what he would like to do, he has a vision of a cathedral, but he cannot incarnate it, because all these Chapter people, and in particular the Precentors, are not there to embody his vision. They have visions of their own. So there is this cost in frustration of seeing what he wants to do, and having very often an enormous amount of wisdom in what he sees needs to be done, but not having the power to create it.

To get things done you have to be political. We can't change the political realities, we've got to live with them. I find it, in fact, very painful indeed to live with them. But that's the particular little bit of world we've got ourselves in, and we've got to be men of God in that.

Rex, the Subdean, is the only person in the Chapter who is politically street-wise, and knows how to get things done. It means that when he is not there, he's sadly missed, because he does have an understanding of how structures work and how things can actually be achieved. In that sense he can come between the Precentor and the Dean to work out a *modus vivendi.*

The Chancellor has generally got something very valuable to say, but you must wait for it. And quite often we don't wait for it, because he is usually thinking along behind us a bit, and when the subject comes to an end and we've moved on to another, John comes up with his little bit of gold nugget. And it's a little bit too late.

Technically, the Dean doesn't have any levers of his own to pull; the levers are in the hands of the different members of the Chapter. So if the Dean wants to spend £1,000 on something, the Treasurer of the Chapter would have to agree with that. If the Dean wanted to have a particular kind of liturgy, the Precentor would have to agree with that. If the Dean wanted to have something done in the library, the Chancellor would have to agree with that. So you see, he has very little that is of his own. A majority vote does work for some things, but the Precentor can act in a very stalling way. The Chapter might vote that the Precentor *should* do something, but that doesn't mean to say that the Precentor *will* do it, especially if he conscientiously thinks that it shouldn't happen. It's very often not only the Precentor who is against the Dean; it's the rest of the Chapter who will disagree with him.

So he is powerless, and nothing happens unless he takes, as he very often does, at least on small issues, and sometimes on big ones, unilateral action in order to shift a log jam. As a tiny example, he wanted to put some carpeting under the Sempringham Pots in the retrochoir, but he knew quite well that the Chapter would never agree to it. So he got hold of the joiner, and said, 'Look, do this, will you?' And he did it. Chapter has not taken it well – we shall have it pulled out as soon as we can.

I, too, have no power at these meetings, I have no levers either. In a sense that gives me a certain kind of detachment, which is useful in terms of balance and maintaining equilibrium, but I sometimes wish I wasn't there because there is nothing for me to do except go along and listen to these chaps arguing. I laugh a lot, yes, I laugh a lot – that's my chief role maybe.

When I first experienced the Cathedral, it was a very unwelcoming place, nothing very much happened in it, not even very many visitors. It wasn't a place where you felt welcome; it was a place where this mysterious choir sang to not very many people. It was very much a closed place to the city, and when Oliver came, he, as it were, threw open its doors to all and sundry, and he has created this enormously active community with all kinds of associations attached to it, and with a much deeper and better relationship with the city and the county – and he did this in the teeth of his Chapter.

IAN LLOYD, MASTER BELL-RINGER

WHEN people meet you for the first time and they ask what hobbies you have, and you say, 'I ring bells', you inevitably get all the old jokes churned out: 'Oh, you like ringing the changes' or 'Been dropping another clanger have you?' and all that! You've heard them all before and I say, 'Yeah, yeah, yeah.' Of course, when it comes down to it, people are actually quite interested once you have got over that sort of initial thing.

I'm an outsider to Lincoln. I moved here with the firm in 1983. You find that bell-ringing is a nice fraternity. As a stranger you can just wander into any town and say, 'I'm a ringer, can I have a ring?' and they want to know where you come from and all the rest of it, which is handy, because I've moved half a dozen times with the Norwich Union. The Norwich Union's like a lot of organizations: it's sort of ask you on Friday, tell you on Monday, and start a week the following Monday. There's obviously an overlap of three or four months before the family move up, so the bell-ringing means I've got something to do every night, and people welcome you with open arms.

I'm manager of the Norwich Union here in Lincoln. I was in Norwich before, and I knew that the next move was going to be into management, which meant either running my own show, as I am in Lincoln, or going into a main branch, at number three. That would have meant moving into a big city, and you have visions of Glasgow or Manchester or Birmingham, one of those frightening sort of places. So when somebody said, 'Would you like to be the manager of Lincoln?' it was, 'Yes, please, what time's the next train leaving?' Mind you, I had to look on the map to see where it was.

At that stage the bypass to Lincoln was not built. The only way you could get into Lincoln from Norwich was all the way up the Newark Road, and, of course, the only thing you can see in front of you is this huge great building stuck on a hill. I remember looking at that and thinking, 'My God, what a fantastic place.' I had no idea at that stage I was going to be a ringer at the Cathedral, because the amount of twelve-bell ringing that I had done was not that great – most of my past ringing had been done on rings of six and eight bells – and certainly I had no pretensions of becoming master, or anything like that, although I'd been tower captain at the last two places I'd been.

After having rung for two and a half, three years, the existing master decided he had had enough and wanted to pack it up. At the Annual General Meeting nobody was more amazed than me when someone put my name forward, which is, obviously, as far as I'm concerned, a very great honour, this being the oldest established Company of Ringers in the country – we go back to 1612. Perhaps I ought to rephrase that and say we're the oldest established company where our existence can be proved to have been continuous; there is evidence of older companies, but these have long since become defunct, so we're the oldest continuous company since 1612.

The thing that's a little bit peculiar here is that you've got this huge, massive central tower that contains Great Tom, the hour bell, but the actual ringing bells are in the south-west tower, St Hugh's Tower, which is the right-hand one of the two towers at the West End.

Well, let me tell you the history of the bells. The back eight, or the heavier eight, they're the bells that were put in in 1913, and replaced an older ring of eight that had been there for some time and were in poor condition. Four more bells, the top four, were added in 1928. So that gave us the ring of twelve. During the early 1920s a lot of strengthening work was done, and a lot of the concrete beams that are in the tower are, in fact, very early examples of pre-cast concrete. From a historical point of view it's quite interesting to see these concrete beams – it would be well worth your while to come and have a visit.

There's always a lot of argument about the relative qualities of old bells and new bells, but the problem with old bells is tuning. The original founders knew little about how to properly tune a bell; all they could do was to tune the bass note. But if you listen to a modern bell, you have got a bass note and you've got harmonics that go with it, which is an octave below, an octave above, and then a third, a fifth, and a dominant seventh. These bells are pretty good; oh yes, they're a superb ring of twelve.

There are other towns that are more popular, somewhere like St Mary, Redcliffe, Bristol or Exeter Cathedral, something like that; they are the top notch. But if you were saying rings of twelve in the country, what would be your top ten? I would say Lincoln would probably come about sixth or seventh in terms of quality. So it wouldn't be a Rolls Royce, but it would certainly be something, shall we say, akin to an Audi – you know, a quality car.

You can ring with a minimum of three people if you want, but it's all down to how many changes you can ring; in other words, how interesting does it become? If you're ringing four bells, for the sake of argument, the number of changes you can ring is 1 × 2 × 3 × 4 – which will give you twenty-four changes. That's the maximum number you can rearrange before you repeat. And on five bells, it's 1 × 2 × 3 × 4 × 5, which gives you 120; six will give you 720; seven bells will give you 5,040; eight will give you 40,320, and so on until you get to twelve, which will give you 479 million!

The prime objective of us being there is to ring for Sunday service, of course, and the object of practice night on Thursday is to improve the standard of those with not so much experience and to improve the overall standard of ringing for service. But within the band we have people of varying abilities, so for the more advanced ringers, we try to ring something a little bit more complicated to keep their minds occupied. If you're ringing the same old thing week in, week out, people get bored. It's a bit like an orchestra if you like: if the most experienced members of the orchestra have to keep playing the *Messiah* every Christmas, they get fed up to the back teeth with it. But if you give them, shall we say, a modern piece that is a lot more difficult, then they get stuck into it.

There's sixteen in the company officially, but we do get quite a few visitors for practice nights and on Sundays, so sometimes you'll end up with maybe twenty people in tow. There's all sorts of ages and occupations. We've got a dental technician, we've got a publicity officer from the county council, we've got an engineer, a teacher, we've got an electronics expert and two or three retired people. Jack Millhouse, he's well over 80, and he's been a member of the company for years. The youngest, I suppose that would be Judith, who's at university, she's 19. We've got five women who are members of the company.

After we had been married for three years, my wife got to the stage of 'if you can't beat 'em, join 'em', and she came out and learnt to ring. But she's packed up since she had the children and never really gone back to it. She's quite happy being a ringing widow; she accepted it a long time ago – I've been ringing since before we were married, so I've been ringing thirty years.

I organize the rota, that's my responsibility as Master. I am responsible for organizing the ringing that goes on, who rings what, what methods we ring, when we ring.

Being a master at a cathedral is a very difficult job, there's so much diplomacy involved with it. I mean, there is a hierarchy involved with the Cathedral. Where I was last before I came here was a little village six, ring of six, where you did what you wanted. You didn't have to worry about asking whether this person was all right or that person was all right; if you wanted to do anything, you just went and saw the vicar, and he said if it was all right, and you just did it. But here there are so many people, so many organizations involved – you've got stewards, you've got organists, you've got choirs, you've got roof tours – you've got all sorts of things that you have to discuss before you can do anything; it's just entirely different.

I suppose I've got an advantage in that I run a business, therefore I'm used to organization. I'm used to getting people to do what I want them to do – and getting them to do it because they want to do it, not because I've told them. And because I'm used to doing that, I find that job relatively easy. But it can be very, very difficult. You have to think about who you've got to clear your decks with.

At a normal tower attendance is a problem, but you tend to find that people are a little bit more committed with the Cathedral, plus the fact that we do get paid, believe it or not. It's something silly, like five pence for every time you turn up, but if you don't turn up you can get fined, so there is a little bit more, how can I put it, a bit more formality about being a member of the Cathedral company than being attached to a lot of other towers. There's a book on the table that comes out, and there's always a bit of backchat 'look how many fines *you've* got', you know the sort of thing. While I'm not saying people come in order to avoid having an 'F' written against their name, it just seems to have a little bit more of something about that, rather than if there was no such register kept.

We take on anybody who wants to learn. You can't really judge their capabilities for a few weeks because there's two distinct aspects to it. There's the physical thing first of all, because it's quite an art in catching the rope and getting the timing right and everything like that. That's the one side of it. Then you move on from there to the theory side, to see whether you have the nous, for want of a better word, to be able to realize what's going on and pick up the methods. (We don't ring tunes, we ring methods, which are the mathematical permutations, if you like.) It takes a fair while to get a ringer up to a reasonable standard starting from scratch. It can take a couple of years. It's not something you can say, I'll start this week and I'll have learnt it all by a week tomorrow.

We're very competitive: there are a lot of what we call striking competitions. We have a Lincoln Diocesan Guild of Ringers and all the towers in Lincolnshire are affiliated to that. The guild itself is divided into four geographical areas; we are in the Central Branch, and there's twenty-odd towers in that. The Central Branch has its own striking competition. The winners of that hold a competition against the winners of the striking competitions from the other branches in the guild, and we then have a guild striking competition, which takes place in May – and which the Cathedral won last year. You'll have maybe half a dozen teams coming from all over the place – Boston,

Swineshead, up as far as Gainsborough – turning up at a particular tower. Then you draw lots to see in which order you're going to ring. We have a judge who's completely independent, who has no idea who the bands are or what order they're ringing in, and he'll give each band so many faults, depending on whether they rang what they were supposed to, whether the ringing was of a good standard or poor standard, or whatever. The team with the lowest number of faults wins the cup. We're in the final for this year as well.

A strong entry usually comes from Saxilby, who are in the Northern Branch, although they're only six miles from Lincoln, and they're usually our closest competition. But because Lincolnshire's such a big county you always get the unknown ones from down in the south of the county. You can get someone turn up from the Elloe Deaneries, which is down near Spalding, and they're a bit of an unknown quantity and you never know what they're going to be like. But you could probably put money on the Cathedral to win this year, and I'm not saying that in a big-headed way.

I find the inside of the church is not as interesting and as fantastic as upstairs. This is an area of the Cathedral the ordinary man in the street never gets to see, but when you go inside that roof, I find it absolutely incredible to think that all that was built 600, 700 years ago by sheer hard labour, no mechanical devices or anything like that. The roof structure is fantastic. It's just a mass of timber. You're talking about timbers that are a foot square, and some of them twenty feet long. If you've ever tried to lift a twenty-foot long, foot-cubed oak – it's a hell of a weight. There must be hundreds of thousands of tons in weight up there, all got up there through sheer manpower.

I certainly wouldn't say I'm an atheist by any manner of means, but I don't go to church because I don't get any satisfaction from going to a church service. I have this constant internal fight. I feel a lot of bitterness about religion when I look at what goes on around the world, because it seems to be 90 per cent of the problems of the world are based upon religion of one sort or another, and that causes me a lot of aggravation. But I certainly find that that building makes me stop and think and say, 'Well, are you absolutely sure you've got it right?' I mean, you look at a building as beautiful as our Cathedral, and you say, 'Well, if that's what religion is about . . .'

JEAN LORD,
VOLUNTEER CO-ORDINATOR

MY husband works in a bank, so consequently we moved around. When we left Yorkshire, where we're from originally, we went to Nottingham, and from Nottingham we came here. My husband came home one day and said, 'We're going to Lincoln, I've got a job there', and everybody dissolved into tears: 'We're not going . . .', 'I don't want to go to Lincoln', 'There's no way I'm going to live in Lincoln, I don't want anything to do with Lincoln at all.' That was fourteen years ago.

The Cathedral looked big and austere, and I didn't really like big buildings. I liked small, comfortable sort of churches, not great, vast buildings like this, and it never really appealed to me at all. I didn't know anybody here, had no connections with anyone, so I didn't particularly like it, and it took me a long time to get used to it.

When we came it was a bad time for housing. Prices had just shot up and we just couldn't find anywhere to live; it was ever so difficult. And it certainly wasn't easy to get to know people in this area either, because, of course, people that live round about have been here for ever and have known each other for a long time, so it was difficult to get involved.

The Lincolnshire character is quite reserved. Once you get past that reserve, then they really are very friendly and genuine, and they accept you very well. But to get to know them is very difficult.

My husband was getting on fine because of his job. He was all right. I did everything I could to get involved, but, even so, it didn't work. I went to church events, Women's Fellowship and night classes and all those sorts of things, and then in the end I got a job, something I'd never done before, just to get out and get involved. It was with children in playschools. Eventually I came to work part time in the Cathedral shop, and ended up by helping to run the shop, by which time I had really begun to get involved in the Cathedral properly.

Eventually I decided I had to leave the shop because we had a lot of things going on at home, the two youngsters were getting married and all sorts of things. So I said I would like to help in some way in the Cathedral. By this time the reception area had been set up, and I asked the Dean if I could do something about getting volunteers involved in the Cathedral. So that's what I started to do, and I took on the role of collecting volunteers, talking to them and encouraging them to come and work here.

A lot of the volunteers, I've found, come to the Cathedral because they need something to do. They all have their different needs, you know. I perhaps need it because my family have grown up and I need something to replace all that busy-ness that I've lost.

There are all kinds of people working here, and the whole place is much more alive and much more used, a much warmer place than it was. When we first came here it really was bleak and unfriendly, people didn't talk to you. But it's changed out of all recognition. A lot of visitors say there's such a wonderful, warm feeling about the place; it's obviously well-used, it's cared for, people are friendly and all that kind of thing.

I enjoy sitting in the choir for evensong. I love the music. Our choirboys sound so wonderful, they fill the Cathedral with sound. It spoils it for everywhere else when you've heard the music in the Cathedral. It's just lovely and warm to be there somehow.

There's a notice as you come in which says 'On entering the Cathedral you will be encouraged to give a donation of £1' – something to that effect. Visitors have read that before they get inside, so they know pretty well what to expect. If you stand away from the reception area, people just walk past. So our presence is to welcome them – and to get money out of them.

My technique is just to talk to people. I stand there at the desk, and if they're going to walk past without digging into their pockets, I say, 'We do have a chest for donations if you would like to leave one.' And if they say 'I'll do it later', that's fine; what more can you do? But I think to certain kinds of people you just have to say, 'Would you like to leave a donation?' – you've got to be as positive as that.

I think older people will give, because they've always been used to giving to a church and they're quite happy to give. You get people who are coming for a day out on a coach, they're not so bothered about giving; you've got to prise money out of them. They've paid for their coach trip, they've paid for their tea – they're not going to give anything to go in a church, because they don't really think of it as a church, it's just another building on a day out. People who're coming to stay in Lincoln, they're usually people who are on holiday and touring about, and they're always prepared to give money, and you don't have to badger them.

Italians are quite generous, Americans are always generous. Germans are not, basically because they don't expect to pay to go into a church; I think their historic buildings are subsidized. You can't get money out of French people. Anyone who has anything to do with the Cathedral says that the French are the most badly behaved – whatever aspect of human behaviour it is, the French are the worst!

EFFIE MANSFIELD, SWITCHBOARD OPERATOR

WE moved up here when my husband retired, roughly four years ago. We wanted to get out of the South-east, which had become much too busy for us. We didn't intend to come here in the first instance – Yorkshire was our first choice – but we came back one time through Lincoln and fell in love with it.

Neither of us had visited the Cathedral before. It was a miserable wet day, but we were so impressed by the Cathedral, and thought how wonderful it would be to live near a cathedral such as that, and so it progressed from there. We kept coming up and liked it more each time.

It didn't take us very long to settle, because we moved into a very friendly neighbourhood. Of course, I hadn't got anything to do with the Cathedral then. That happened purely by chance. A friend who belongs to our church was working as a volunteer at the Cathedral and told me there was a part-time job coming up, which I thought sounded fascinating. To have lived in Lincoln for less than a year and to be going for a job at the Cathedral! And I went for an interview and got it.

It's the job that the three of us share together – the other two are Rita Simpson and Jo Keedy. The job is telephonist/secretary in the Communications Office. It's a new system. They didn't have a switchboard at all until this switchboard was installed, so I suppose things weren't very efficient.

We get very varied calls. The normal business calls, which we route through to people, and some funny calls really: the name of Tennyson's dog,* we've been asked for that several times; times

*There is a statue of Tennyson, with his dog, Karenina, outside the Chapter House, which is on the east side of the Cathedral.

of services, that's a very common one; questions about the age of the Cathedral; different aspects of the architecture, which we can't deal with, but we can put the calls to the people who do know; and questions about organists, the dates particular organists worked here, such as William Byrd and people like that.

I suppose you could call it a public information service. I think the Cathedral plays such a big part in people's lives in Lincoln and Lincolnshire that they ring us up, and we're very pleased to help them. We always try to answer with a smile in our voice, 'Lincoln Cathedral, good morning' or 'good afternoon'.

The three of us all get along very well, we see each other outside work too. It is fortunate we get on – you should see our office, it's very, very small. We have people coming in, and when there are more than four people, it's really crowded. We are going to decorate it for Christmas this year. Rita suggested it. Last year we bought a gift each and put them in a bag, so we all gave one and received one, rather than give three and receive three. I gave a piece of something lacy from the Lace Shop, if I remember rightly, and I picked out perfumed drawer liners.

John and I belong to our local church, and I sing in the choir there. I am quite a religious person; I would say I have a strong faith. It's the village church of Nettleham we go to. It's a lovely old church, parts of it are thirteenth-century, I believe – there's no guidebook at the moment. Jo belongs to that church and sings in the choir as well.

Rita doesn't belong to any church, but she is absolutely crazy about the Cathedral – she really is, she just loves the Cathedral. And she says from time to time, 'I do love working here.' You know, we often say, 'To think that we work here'; we still say this three years on. We have our off days when things go wrong and the switchboard plays up, but we all love the job.

I come into work through the West Front. In the morning it's all quiet and semi-dark, and the still sort of hits you. I always think what a tremendous building this is, there's a sense of awe still, even though I do it nearly every morning. And it's just a splendid feeling to think, 'Gosh, *I* work here,' and all these centuries ago people worked here before me.

We can see the towers from our garden, and sometimes we go out in the evening just to see the towers lit. Quite often John says, 'Well, I never thought that I'd live so near a marvellous cathedral.'

We have two children: 28 our son is now, and Rosemary is 24. Rosemary's in High Wycombe and Alistair's in London, but they like it very much here, and they both come up for Christmas. They think it's a lovely place.

LYNDON MATTHEWS, POLICE CONSTABLE

I COME from a place called Consett, which is in County Durham, so I'm a Wearsider, South Tyne, you see. In 1973 I joined the Lincolnshire police. I wanted to get away from Durham, from parents and things like that, get a bit of independence. I found it very relaxed, and different altogether to where I'd lived. Consett was a heavy industrial area at that time, there was steel in the town, and it was a very, very dirty place. I found Lincoln quieter, cleaner. I also found that the people weren't as openly friendly towards you as they are up in my native north-east, but the place itself I was quite taken with.

I did roughly three years on town duties at Gainsborough, then I had a rural beat in Saxilby. From Saxilby I applied for the Dog Section, and I remained there for four years, until I came here. Two years ago, Easter Monday, I got this area, the Bailgate area, to work as a resident beat. My job is to get to know folk, and them to get to know me, and to work as a community policeman. And it's worked, I might say. I get on very well with the vast majority of people and I think they get on with me.

My beat starts at Motherby Lane, which is opposite the police station more or less. Then you come up Steep Hill and it takes in, to the west, Union Road, to the north it goes as far as Newport Arch, and to the east it goes Eastgate traffic lights, Priory Gate, down Lindum Road, on to Danesgate and then across again.

I get on very well with the Dean of the Cathedral. We have met on a number of occasions. I have his authority to go into the Cathedral and have a stroll around and see that there's no minor mischief, and assist the vergers and anyone else who has a vested interest in maintaining the peace and the tranquillity in the Cathedral. It doesn't get many problems. Occasionally you do get one or two who go in and try the offertory boxes and things like that; it's inevitable when you've got a mass number of people going through.

I sometimes go into the building on my own at very quiet times. It's not unusual to see me in the building at seven o'clock in the morning just for five or ten minutes. I believe in religion being a personal thing, you see, I'm not one for outwardly showing it. I go in there if things are getting on top of me, and just have a quiet reflection in one of the chapels or just stand in the nave and think. I find it very relaxing, very peaceful, and then I get things in perspective.

From time to time when things are going on within the Cathedral, like, for example, when they've had the Hallé Orchestra, I've stood in the back and heard them play, or carol services at Christmas, for example, that sticks in my mind – it's fantastic, the atmosphere is terrific.

I do love this building, I think it's a magnificent building. How they managed to build it all those years ago, I don't know; and it's stood the test of time fairly well, hasn't it?

In addition to myself, we've got a minimum of one other foot officer who would work up here, and, of course, you've got the car, what we call the IRV – that's Instant Response Vehicle. That's usually a chap called PC Currie, although if he's away for some reason, then somebody else would drop into that slot.

I would say there'd be no shortage of people in the Force who would want my job. Because it is a nice area, there's nice people, moderate-thinking people who are not extreme in any sense of the word. They realize the rules are there for the betterment of everybody.

I don't like talking about class, it's a bit alien to me. I like to think that the majority of people are right-thinking people. I think it's perhaps upbringing; they realize up here that the police service is there to help them in the main, despite maybe on one or two occasions when they've crossed swords, as it were, by committing minor indiscretions. I don't believe that I've got many criminals in my area. Of course, these days anyone can commit a minor indiscretion, for example, with a motor vehicle – you know, simply leaving your car engine running while you nip into the shop.

There's certain areas you go into and the very fact that you're wearing this uniform means open hostility towards you; it doesn't matter who's inside that uniform, they see this uniform and that's it, and you could come to some grief in certain areas. Well, that doesn't apply round here. So you learn that not all individuals are against you, which is a big thing. I would say my life has changed coming up here. I believe the job that I'm doing is worthwhile, because people here think it's worthwhile; it goes hand-in-glove. If you're doing a job where you're constantly seen as an enemy, it wears thin and you think, what am I doing the job for?

There's times when the Cathedral's come into my dreams, when I've been thinking about the job or my subconscious has been thinking about work. Kids' pedal cycles are the bane of my life. They just do not conform to the rules and regulations – they have no lights on them, a lot of them don't have any brakes on them – and in this dream I try to stop as many as I can. I'm on the south side of the Cathedral trying to stop somebody who swerves round me and carries on.

KATIE MIDDLETON, VERGER

I'M from Lincoln itself. My father was a builder; he had his own company until he died. And my mother brought us all up, five of us. We were quite a handful. Mum would say to the older boys, 'Oh, take them to the Cathedral.' It was a place to go on a rainy afternoon, and if it was fine, we would go up the tower. So we knew it quite well. We knew all the corners, we knew where the Imp was and all the interesting little carvings; it was a sort of playground really. We didn't come to services here because it was always a bit snooty, or we thought so.

It was in my last year at university that I thought I wanted to be a verger. It just grew on me, and I was quite determined that was what I wanted to do. It's just something I wanted to do, I don't think I could explain it. Possibly I chose the job subconsciously, as a way of accompanying my faith, the desire to serve the Church in a secular way.

We run the place. We're the housekeepers if you like. We open up in the morning and lock up at night. We prepare services, we officiate at services, we make sure it's generally tidy and clean, and just generally keep an eye on things and make sure everything runs smoothly.

First of all in the morning I unlock all the doors and I walk around the cloisters, but I open the cloisters last of all. Then I look up at the big tower from the north side. It's lovely if the sun's shining, but if it's misty, you can see only half of the tower, but you can see the kestrels and the pigeons and the blackbirds. We had a blackbird's nest in the cloisters and we watched the baby ones grow up.

You've got to be able to work long hours, and you've got to be quite strong. If we have to put all the chairs out in the nave, for example, it's an entire day of physically hard work. There are 2,000 chairs. You have to be able to deal with people, you have to be quite patient and tolerant: people asking for things, 'Where's this?' 'Where's that?' Occasionally you'll get somebody who disapproves very strongly of having to pay at the West Door and you have to try to justify it to them; or somebody's lost something and you have to find it or tell them you can't find it; or there's an accident and you have to deal with that, distribute aspirins or put a plaster on somebody's knee, or whatever. So it's quite wide-ranging what we do for people. There's a lot of walking involved. You have to wear flat, thick-soled shoes to cope with the stone floors.

Everybody thinks I'm a deaconess or trained for the ministry in some way. They never know what I am! I think they probably have less problem with the men, because a male verger is more usual. They usually come up to me and say, 'Excuse me, would you mind telling me what you are?' I found it a bit disconcerting at first, but you get used to it. I think it's good wearing a cassock because people can spot us from a long way off and they can see that it's somebody official, and it sets us apart. On Sundays and special services we wear a blue cassock, with a white jabot, which is like a sort of neckcloth. Otherwise we wear black gowns and white gloves; very smart, don't you know. We like to think we're the best turned-out cathedral vergers.

Whenever I go to another town, I always go to the cathedral and do a little bit of spying. They all wear different clothes and have different colours. Truro, for example, wears red cassocks for special occasions; Salisbury wears green; Westminster Abbey – they wear black, but they have a colour on their gown. There's little variations from place to place, but Lincoln's the only one that wears pale blue, it's the Lincoln colour.

If we are standing by the organ and we see a party coming to the West End, we can usually tell straightaway what nationality they are. The French are the worst, you know; they come pouring in, shrieking and shouting, they don't put any money in the boxes and the children are all over the place. Italians all talk very loud; Spaniards tend to as well. Scandinavians are very good usually; they're quite interested and quiet. Of course, these are vast generalizations.

The locals come in for some peace and quiet or to show visitors around. But they usually come on Sunday morning, when half the Cathedral is shut off because of services, and they want to look around and don't understand that they can't. They're sometimes a bit awkward, which is frustrating for us. They say, 'We live locally, why can't we go here?' And we think, well, if they live locally, why don't they come in at another time when there isn't a service on?

Sometimes, early in the morning, when there's nobody else in the Cathedral and it's nice and peaceful, you think, 'I gain from the peace and quiet.' Just before a big service when we're all running round like scalded chickens, I wonder what it's all for.

It's much more relaxed and restful in the winter. I always feel people who come to the Cathedral in winter are people who want to come. We don't get these big coach parties who are just hopping from one place to another. And I suppose it's more friendly in a way.

There's a very definite hierarchy among vergers. I started off as Fourth Verger, which is the lowest of the low here. I then became Beadle Verger, who is in charge of the choir, and I am now Canon's Verger, which is second in command. Above that is Dean's Verger, who basically runs the place.

Roy's my direct boss; he's great. He expects a lot from us, we have to work hard for him and the standard has to be high, but he's very fair about it. I get on very well with him as a person, which helps. If it isn't just as he wants it, he'll let you know. He's very conscious he's Dean's Verger, and he's the boss, really in the whole Cathedral, and he likes to keep that position, which is fair enough, and he's very good at it. Several people outside the Cathedral have said to me that it's a much nicer place to come to since he's been here. We've got a very happy team at the moment and we all get on with each other.

It depends on what time of day it is as to which part of the

Cathedral I like best. Early in the morning I like the Gilbert candles at the East End. I like the south-east transept very much, that's where the choir vestry is. Sometimes I just stand in a little corner somewhere and feel that's a special corner at that particular time. It's a very living place, and it calls people to come into it by its position on the hill and by the external appearance of it. Within the Cathedral itself, all the people who work there form quite a close-knit community, which again draws people in.

We do work very long hours, so the job is bound to dominate your life. When I was still living at home it was the be-all and end-all of my existence, which at the time was what I wanted, but I think since I got married, it's not dominated quite so much.

I met my husband, who's a lay clerk, before I started working here. He was sharing a house with my sister's boy-friend at the time, and then through just always being in the same place together, it grew from that – he would be in the Cathedral once or twice, three times a day, singing in the choir, and he'd pop into the vergers' office, and he'd wink at me from the choir stalls.

I suppose the romance was noticed by all the others in the Cathedral and I think they were quite pleased to see it going on, because it was so unusual. If you think about it, previously when vergers have got involved with lay clerks, it's usually ended in disgrace. And I think people liked it because it was all in-house, rather nice to have all happened within the Cathedral.

This may sound silly, but if you're away at all, on holiday or something, you do miss the building ever so much. When we went for our honeymoon, we were away for a fortnight. It was the longest I've been away from it since I started, and after it was over, as we got closer to Lincoln, we were shouting, 'Where is it? Where is it? *There* it is, on the hill!' And do you know, when I got back the first thing I had to do was to go in and make sure it was still all right.

I know my Mum's very proud of me. She likes to see me in my blue cassock and white gloves leading processions and that. My little nephews like coming in and seeing me, and it makes them feel very important if they can go up and speak to a verger and be shown little things that other people don't see. To give them a treat I take them up into the Chapter House roof or into a chapel that's kept locked up, or they'll come into the kitchen downstairs, past the door marked 'Private', which is quite exciting when you're only 4.

TERRY MILLWARD, LAY CLERK

IN the old days it was very much Uphill and Downhill: the Cathedral and environs were Uphill, and the working men lived down below. You only have to look over the edge of the cliff and you can see the working-class streets, which were built for the workers at the forges and the steelworks down below. That gap has now decreased an awful lot, but I think it is still very much a city on two levels. A lot of people in this bottom half of the city have no reason to come up here at all in their day-to-day business. Mind you, a large number of Lincoln people have never been to London. It's a very isolated town in an isolated county, which is part of its fascination for me.

I was a journalist on the *Surrey Advertiser* in my youth, did all the things people on local papers do, decided it wasn't for me, and so I went to Durham University, late, at 21, and did my degree. I got my first chance at teaching singing in Durham for a few years; then I went to Bristol, which I didn't like very much – too big for me, I like the smaller towns. In those days you could get a teaching job almost at thc drop of a hat; it wasn't the same as now. So I came to Lincoln, found they wanted a tenor, liked the place, thought I'd sing in the choir, even though the Cathedral lay clerk's salary in those days was the princely sum of £300 a year – and you couldn't live on that even in 1972. But I found a teaching job in a school just five miles out of Lincoln. I've been very lucky because the school has grown as I've been there, and I've managed to get promotions within the school, so I haven't had to look around. It's an ideal situation, living in a small city and teaching in the country.

When we first came up to Lincoln, up through North Hykeham on the A46, my wife said, 'Good God, this is awful', because it's not very inspiring down there. But it gradually got better and better as we got higher. I'm fairly used to cathedrals, having sung in Durham, which is fairly big, but getting out of the car and standing underneath the south side of the Cathedral, it really was quite stupendous. Nowadays I don't give the place a second thought. In a way one tends to use it as a factory – it's awful to say – being a lay clerk and coming in and out of it every day. But it was stupendous at first. And yet, although it's so big, it's a friendly building. It's not like Liverpool, which I dislike intensely because it's so lacking in personality.

The first sight of Lincoln from the bottom was pretty ghastly, but on the other hand the city wouldn't be complete without the bottom bit as well, in that it adds to it. It's not like Salisbury, it's not like Winchester, they're almost too perfect, I couldn't bear to live there. Lincoln's got a real heart to it, it's got a bit of metal to it, literally and metaphorically. It's not a northern city, but it's got a sort of northern feel to it in its architecture, and in its individuality too. I like a city with guts – good God, we've got a fourth-division football team, which I go and watch when I can. I love it.

It all depends on the cathedral's foundation as to what choristers are called. At York they call them songmen, which is rather descriptive; here they're called lay vicars or lay clerks. What happened was, in the Middle Ages the services were sung by the priest vicars themselves, and in the end, either through idleness, absenteeism or inability, their places in the choir were taken by laymen. They might or might not be religious, but nowadays they are in fact semi-professional musicians doing a day-to-day job, which most of us do just because we love doing it; we do it for love really and get peanuts even now, £1,500 a year. It's hard work and you wouldn't do it if you didn't take it seriously and love doing it. It's a real commitment, especially for ones with families, because it's every weekend while we're in term, and one might as well take one's bed there for Christmas and Easter.

I don't know what inspires me to do it. I don't think any of us can say exactly what it is. It's a combination of various things. I've been involved in Church music since I was a boy, and most of us have got a religious background. I think most of us have a faith, but it might not always be an Anglican faith particularly. Obviously the music inspires us. The building inspires us. It's certainly not the publicity, or the fame, or the audiences – you should try a Tuesday evensong in February sometimes, when the temperature in the bloody place is about 32 degrees and there's about one old lady and a dog!

It's a combination of that indefinable thrill that goes up and down one's back, a feeling that it's been done for so long, that one's part of a great long line of history, and there's always a hope that it is offering something worthwhile and inspiring people, helping them to relax and think and meditate.

Like all groups of people, we have our differences. At the moment we've a choir of younger men, and as senior lay clerk, it's been my job to try to sort of mould people together. We've had one or two upsets, obviously, as you do with one or two young men coming in who are perhaps a bit insecure, not quite sure where they're going, not quite sure what the standards are. But on the whole, I think we get on extremely well. Certainly we seem to drink beer together quite well!

I've only recently met the new organist. I don't know what he'll be like, I don't make any predictions anymore. I've heard that he's very good, but one just doesn't know, one has to wait and see what he's like on the floor with us. He's got to prove himself to us, just as we've got to prove ourselves to him.

Something that we've been introduced to recently is quite a lot of modern music, which we haven't done before, and we enjoy doing that. I think we started off with a little bit of hesitancy, but now we attack it with a lot of zest, and I think, to our surprise, we've pulled it off. We were tending to speed up on the psalms recently; it's only my opinion, but I like to do them fairly slowly and thoughtfully, and they did tend to go at a fair pace. But we've slowed them down and they've become more thoughtful again.

The acoustics are not as good as you might think, mainly because of the woodwork; there's an immense amount of woodwork around the choir. And of course, the stalls are so far apart – the two sections of the choir are further apart than anywhere else in England; you almost have to wave a red flag to attract the attention of the other side. I've found if I've gone and sung in more intimate cathedrals, like Southwell and Peterborough, you get immediate satisfaction from the acoustics, which we don't in Lincoln, but that's a very minor matter. I don't really think about acoustics very much, I just get on and do the job.

THE REVEREND JULIET MONTAGUE, DEACON

I GREW up in a world that was very much an adult world, a sort of commune type family, with my grandparents, my parents, my brother and my sister, and me as the only child amongst all that. I was the youngest, my brother and sister being pre-war and me being decidedly post-war because my father was away for a long time.

It was very much a rural childhood, we were very cut off. It was a village that was one and a half miles from the nearest bus, and we had a smallholding with something like seven cows and 2,000 chickens, odds and ends like that. It was a totally irreligious childhood. None of my family want to church at all, although my grandfather in his younger days had sung in the church choir and been a bell-ringer.

I had very little contact with the Church until I was in my teens. I became involved then because we got a new vicar who was young and energetic – very untypical for a village – who had been a youth chaplain in Smethwick of all places, in Birmingham. The coming south nearly killed him because the people were so different and not what he was used to at all, but he and I developed a very good relationship. He was very much a prime influence on my life, because of his enthusiasm more than anything else, his sheer zest for what he was doing, and he gave me something of a good grounding, he started me off.

I wanted to believe, I desperately wanted to believe. I suppose the fact that I had a terrific amount of ill health actually helped me in my wanting to believe. I was born with partial facial paralysis, which meant that I was almost totally blind and deaf on the left side, and had very little movement on that side of my face. That slowly improved, but it involved a lot of hospital visits and treatment to try to strengthen the use of the eye – there was nothing much you could do about anything else.

Then at 9 years old I developed asthma after an attack of measles, and shortly after that was found to have additional bones in my spine, additional vertebrae, which led to curvature. The only reason I say all that is for me they were very significant things in my childhood. At a time when most girls are thinking about developing into young women, I was seeing a deterioration in myself, and I did not know when it would end.

I was attending clinics with youngsters who were in wheelchairs, and I continued to deteriorate roughly between the ages of about 10 and 16, and it presented a lot of problems. It turned me inwards to some extent. I did a lot of thinking about things like fairness and justice, and I think it made me think a lot about the setting right of the scales of justice after death. At that time, in my early teens, I think it was difficult to look further than me for a while, but as I grew older my horizons broadened and I began to think, well if *I* feel like that, how must people feel who grow up in areas of the world where they know nothing of actually living – it's just existing for the first few years of life followed by death.

I wanted to believe that there was some kind of justice, but at the same time I was looking for a reason why I had been singled out to bear what felt to me at the time like pretty huge burdens. My brother was a very strong atheist and we had furious arguments and debates. The family was all like that, we constantly had enormous sort of round the table debates, and we would go on until late into the night about the creation of the world and other such things. There was a lot of food for thought in that way.

My beliefs really changed when I was at teacher-training college and I found myself, quite by accident, swept into the Cambridge Christian Intercollegiate Union, which was one of the most profound experiences of my life, following my initial vicar in my village. The Cambridge Christian Union did more for me than anything else, I think. I went with them to the Round Church at Cambridge, and I was very privileged to be a part of the wonderful Saturday evening Christian Union meetings, where we had wonderful speakers. It was a great thing to be involved in because of the enthusiasm – we practically used to take the roof off when we sang and people were stacked on the stairways and every corner they could get into; they were very eager young Christians. It was a very privileged position to be in.

My health still wasn't good. I had had a very bad time with bronchitis and various related complaints, but I was able to manage with the aid of steroids and other drugs, and I coped. The biggest thing for me at that stage was that I found in the people I got to know at Cambridge a large number of very good friends, several of whom still remain as friends, and I found that the level of acceptance of me was astoundingly great. It was an intoxicating experience, I suppose, because of not having had a whole gang of friends all in one place at an earlier age, and I wanted to be free to enjoy it.

I had a wild couple of years doing all the things I had never been able to do as a child because I wasn't fit enough – things like punting down the River Cam in the middle of the night in the rain, and drinking whisky and eating shortbread in Grantchester meadows at one o'clock in the morning. I would never have been allowed to do that as a child because I was never allowed to do anything that might make me ill. And I did everything. I got drunk, furiously, copiously drunk on some occasions. I did all the things I needed to do to let my hair down, and I felt the change in me, I felt a dramatic change in me.

And then I realized after a couple of years that one couldn't live this sort of life for ever. I had by that time dropped out of college. I got a bread-and-butter job as an executive officer with the Department of the Environment, and I worked for a while in Cambridge, which was really just to keep me independent so that I did not have to go back home. I had an awful fear that if I went back home I would never come away again, and I had to be able to support myself.

In the meantime I had been baptized and confirmed in the Round Church in Cambridge at the age of 19. One important bit to do with my faith at that point was the fact that after about a year it seemed to me that this wonderful ecstatic faith felt so emotionally based – I'm talking about this whole student-based, excited, youthful, energetic sort of faith – that I was uncertain whether it was lasting. It felt like this was a great sort of trip, and I felt I needed to know whether it was something that was going to last through thick and thin. I needed to find out whether I had got the discipline to survive a non-excited sort of faith. Slowly I was coming to the conclusion that there wasn't enough 'meat' in an emotionally based faith, that in some ways it didn't allow me to push far enough with the questions.

So one summer I took myself off to a sleepy little village church, I can't quite remember where it was. And for the whole of one long vac. I went to this church with about six old ladies and an old parson, and it was very, very dead – about as dead as I could find – to do a kind of spiritual exercise to find out whether this faith had to be hyped up for it to be real. And I survived that, it didn't actually go away.

When a friend asked if I would like to come and share a flat in London, it seemed to be just the right move to make. So I went to London and I shared a condemned flat with four men over an old second-hand TV shop in Tooting, south London. The water dripped down the light flex in the bathroom, there were mice in the kitchen, and the windows fell out on more than several occasions; it was really slumming it, but the people I was sharing with were enormous fun. They were all ex-Cambridge, they were old friends, and during that time I was living there they carted me off to church. It was like a crocodile out of school, me marching along between them. We went to the local parish church, which was middle-of-the-road Anglican with a slight tendency towards the Catholic end, but it was my first taste of Catholicism and I liked it, I liked it enormously.

And there I met the next major influential person in my life, who was a brand-new curate from Salisbury Theological College, and a very different type from people I had known before. Colin was an Anglo-Catholic priest, a south London man with very limited education, but a tremendous ability to get alongside people. He was also no stranger to suffering, although not physically, he had had a lot to handle in his life. There was a very good rapport from the word go. Through him I became involved in a lot of the work of the Church: we ran the youth club together, I was in the choir, I was a member of the church council – you name it, I was in it. There was a lot of demand there, because it was bed-sit land and there were a lot of lonely young people, often with enormous problems.

A lot of things happened at that stage. I was adjusting to London life, the Church was taking over more and more of my life, while I was doing a job that was desperately unfulfilling. I think it is true to say that it was the first time in my life, largely through my curate friend Colin – he was capable of allowing me to express my feelings about my physical problems without feeling anxious about it – that I found myself able to be really honest with people about me. That allowed me to come pretty close to a nervous breakdown, and I spent some time at St George's Hospital in London having psychotherapy, the express intention of which was that I should be able to learn to express anger, which I couldn't. I hit the lowest point I think I have ever hit at that point.

I carried on working – I never have had a time when I couldn't – and I spent that time helping to rebuild the church hall, slapping on Cuprinol and doing practical physical things. Learning how to cut templates to fill arches was wonderful physical therapy, and dashing off to the pub at lunch times for a drink was great – it was very much a gin-drinking parish – and, again, it was a rebellious thing to do, to go and knock back the alcohol. I think I learnt to be able to be angry, not so much with people, but with God, and I think my faith took on a different tone altogether. It wasn't this sort of 'up' all the time. I had actually discovered the depths and grown up through them, and

I discharged myself after a year's psychotherapy. I suppose in a way I was going through a sort of delayed adolescence, that all the things that had been repressed came out in my early twenties.

It was after maybe three years in London that I voiced my feelings about being drawn towards the Church as a full-time vocation, as a life's work. And Colin said to me, 'I wondered when you were going to come up with something like that. I thought you would sooner or later.' I was very hesitant about telling anyone, partly because I thought my family would think I had completely flipped. Here was me, I had been set fair to be an executive officer before the age of 30, I had a good career going for me in a sense, and I knew they would think it was terribly reckless to throw all this away for a 'dead end' like the Church. So that made me nervous for a start and, secondly, I really had very little idea whether they would accept me or not. It was quite a big thing for me at that stage to put myself forward for anything where I might get turned down. In the end I braved it, I ventured forth. I had to do it for the fact that the Church was eating into my life in such a large way that I had very little time for anything else and I was resenting the work I was doing more and more, it was becoming a real ordeal to do it.

I went to see the Bishop's Examining Chaplain, who was a tremendously powerful lady. I can remember the interview still to this day. I felt that I hadn't a hope, that I was absolutely useless. Despite all my pessimism, I was called to ACAM, which is the Advisory Council for the Church's ministry, and I was invited to take part in a three-day selection conference. It was the last of the selection conferences that were purely women – nowadays they do it combined – and there were about twenty of us.

The only reason that I failed my conference was on health grounds. Again my health dogged me. They sent me for several medicals – I had to go to Harley Street on one occasion – and they decided that I was 'too vulnerable to infection to be able to be of any real use' once ordained, because I would spend so much time being ill. And then, in what I can only interpret as a sort of divine intervention – the Bishop of Southwark at that stage was Mervyn Stockwood – and Mervyn Stockwood, who had been ill himself, overruled the ACAM decision, which amazed me, but bishops can do that, they don't have to take notice of their Advisory Councils, and so I was given Southwark's backing for training.

I came here to Lincoln and everything, from the very first moment I set foot over the doorstep, felt right. I felt that if I could manage to hold my health together enough, everything would be all right. I can remember my first sight of the Cathedral; it still gives me a thrill every time I see it. I think the sad thing was that I didn't come up at night, so I didn't see that wonderful sight that I got so familiar with every time that I came into Lincoln from holidays; the Cathedral all lit up and visible from thirty miles away, the beacon that meant you were home. I came up in January, it was six feet deep in snow, and I took a taxi up – I would never have got up Steep Hill otherwise I don't think – and my first interview took place on West Common, ploughing through six-foot-deep snowdrifts, not adequately clad for this kind of weather, because it wasn't like that down south.

Considering it was a part of the country that I had never been to before, I felt immediately drawn to the place; it felt like somewhere where I could be for a long time, and it was going to be a long time.

To do the Bachelor of Theology degree at that stage was four years – I was the last person to take that four-year degree, it's three years now. I remember Henry Richmond saying to me at the end of the interview, 'Do you want time to think about this?' and I said, 'I don't need time, I know now.' I was so certain, and I never ever wavered from that through four years, I was utterly convinced it was the right place to be. I wasn't certain I could do a degree because of the state that I got into before exams, but I knew that if anybody could get me through, they could.

Eighty students, that was all, including the staff; it was more like a large family and it gave me so much that I felt privileged to have. When I went down to chapel in the mornings, I used to think about what I had been doing at that time in London, how I would have been throwing myself down the escalator on to the

Tube along with half a million other lemmings, and how privileged I was to be able to come down for breakfast in this time of space and quiet, privileged to be doing what I wanted to do, to be set free to think about the things I wanted to think about, and it felt like somebody had taken the shackles off me – it felt wonderful.

At the end of my four years I decided that my health had been so much better up here there was no way I could go back to London. Much as I would have liked to have gone back to be near my old friends, I felt that I was going to be more use in an area of the country where I was so much fitter. So I asked to be released from Southwark, and the Bishop gave me my release. He was glad that somebody wanted to come to the northern end of the country rather than wanting to go the other way. And the Bishop of Lincoln took me on at Gainsborough, where I went to work as deaconess with a parish priest who was a canon in the Cathedral, and a curate. I spent four years working there, building up parish experience really. I was very fortunate in having a vicar who believed that the development of one's ministry was very much a personal thing. He did not interfere; he gave me a great deal of freedom to do the things that I wanted to do, to try things out, and we worked very well together.

The way you are turned out from theological college, you have got a fair amount of theory, but when it came to taking services, taking funerals or taking baptisms, you hadn't any practical experience. Most of what I learnt I learnt as a sort of baptism of fire. I did my first funeral about three weeks after I arrived, when the curate and the vicar's holidays had overlapped and I was left in sole charge, and during that time I had five funerals. I had never taken one before in my life, and I just had to get on and do them. I did them with the help of the Co-op funeral directors, who were marvellous; I would never have survived but for them. I did my first baptism on an afternoon when the curate's wife rang up and said, 'There's a family waiting outside the church', and I had to go and do a baptism with no notice at all. But at least I got started, and I just got on with it. I did find a lot of confidence from doing those sorts of things and from finding that, in fact, I didn't need to be quite as nervous as I was.

After a while the curate left, and that led to one of the most painful moments of my life. We got another curate: here was a raw deacon just come to the parish after I had been there a couple of years, and he was immediately ordained priest in the parish church. I hadn't expected it to be a painful moment, because I knew this was going to happen – at least my head knew perfectly well – but I felt a tremendous pang that this could not be me. I hope it wasn't noticeable, because I would not have wanted to do anything to detract from his day in any way, and I don't believe that because one isn't allowed things for oneself one should make life miserable for other people. But that was the first time when I really felt the stirrings of being called to the priesthood. I had thought before that I was perfectly content with my lot. I had taken the view that there were a lot of things that I could do within the vast ministry and that to be niggling about the things I couldn't do was a stupid waste of time, but from that moment I knew that I did actually have a call to the priesthood.

After I had been there about three years, I got a letter saying there was a position as Associate Pastor for the Cathedral, would I be interested to meet the Chapter? The Chancellor was going to be away at that time – I think he was on sabbatical or something – and I was to meet four members of Chapter. I came in fear and trembling, feeling that possibly I was going out of my depth. I knew that the Precentor was certainly not in favour of the priesthood of women and really quite dubious about women in general as far as ministry goes, but that the Subdean was quite deeply involved with the movement for the ordination of women, so I knew I had got mixed feelings among the group. I felt that it was important to establish at that time what all their feelings were. So quite deliberately I asked what they felt about women's ministry. The Precentor said that he hadn't really given it a lot of thought. The Subdean said that it was great, marvellous, they were really looking forward to having a woman permanently on the staff, they had had an American woman priest for nine months before as Associate Pastor and they wanted somebody permanent. The Archdeacon, Christopher Laurence, said he was looking forward to seeing the first woman bishop, and then the Dean came up at the tail-end, and he said, 'It's all very well to get so excited at this, but really we are only just beginning to learn what it means to work with a woman colleague – it's a matter of working it out as we go along.' And I thought that that was one of the most positive, realistic things, and I felt that I wanted to work with a man like that, who recognized that it wasn't necessarily going to be that easy, but it was worth working at, and that made me feel, yes, I want to work here.

My duties are mainly to be responsible for the pastoral care of the congregation. I fulfil a lot of the functions of a vicar. I have on occasions acted as representative for the Dean at events he can't get to. I take a very full part in the liturgy in the worship. I preach, not that frequently, but more frequently than non-residentiary canons, and I think I have as full a part in the life of the Cathedral as I could possibly be allowed to have at this stage, short of celebrating. I cannot celebrate communion, although I can administer the elements. I can't hear confession and I can't give absolution; these are things that only a priest can do.

In May last year it became possible for women to be ordained, and twenty-four of us from this diocese were ordained deacon by Bishop Hardy in the Cathedral. That meant not so much a change in practice, with the exception that we could now take a marriage, but the change from being a lay minister to being an ordained minister meant we could be called the Reverend, sit in Synod, and that one could sit with the clergy in services instead of being set apart.

There are still large areas of the country where they have never seen a woman priest at work; people are not used to the sight of a woman wearing the dog collar and quite often they'll stare. I never take part in a service in the Cathedral without having in the back of my mind that for someone this may be their first experience of having seen a woman taking part, and that if they can go away with the feeling that this has been a good experience, then that is what I want to achieve.

Because so many clergy come through the Cathedral, I inevitably will meet clergy who are going to be strongly opposed to women's ordination. Some refuse the chalice from me because I am a woman. Most however are very polite and it is no problem to accept their view because that is where they have stood for years in many cases. But some are less polite, and it makes me slightly annoyed when I meet people who allow their standards to slip in that way: no matter what their feelings are, they are still duty-bound, as I am, to be polite.

There was one wonderful occasion not long ago when a gentleman was sitting behind the choir during the communion service, and as it was a weekend when there was a conference for women's ministry, it felt relevant to pray for the women who were at that meeting, and during the prayers he was muttering remarks like 'rubbish' and 'nonsense', and our senior lay vicar turned round in the middle of the service, and said 'Do you mind!' It's swings and roundabouts. For every one who is negative and difficult, I find about ten who are supportive and helpful.

This Cathedral is much more than just a building. It has a thriving, living congregation of people, many of whom are deeply thinking people. And, being the Cathedral, it has its share of eccentrics, people who have fallen out with their vicar, and that's why they come here. It's got a very eclectic congregation. It has a congregation that is quite unlike a parish church, and they are the life of that building and they care very deeply about the building. But at times I feel perhaps we care more for the building than for the work that we are supposed to be doing, and that is always a problem when you have got a magnificent edifice like the Cathedral; it's difficult sometimes to see beyond that to the real work that we are about. It feels sometimes as if the building absorbs all the energy that people have and stops them from looking beyond. It needs emphasizing from time to time that this is not really what we are about – it doesn't matter if these stones collapse – that's not the be-all and end-all, and I think that is something that I and all the other clergy need to say.

I think I will always live with the fear of not being quite

adequate for the job, especially as I am working with fellow clergy who are immensely well qualified. I feel constantly, am I really adequate for this task?

At the moment, I am supposed to be off sick with stress, largely because this has been a year of firsts, which have been enormous stresses. The first wedding was a very big stress, partly because the two young people concerned wanted a quiet wedding, but they wanted me to take it, which was a dangerous thing to do with the press interest in women ministers. I had to keep it out of the press at all costs, and I had to get it right for them – because it might be *my* first, but it is *their* only wedding, hopefully.

Prior to that I gave my first lecture at the Theological College. Always in this line of work you are pushing forward frontiers, doing something that you haven't done before and undertaking things that you are not quite sure whether you really are going to make a success of, and that inevitably put slight pressure on me. This time of year has always been a bad time for my asthma anyway, and I had 'flu about a fortnight ago, so I am not coping terribly well at this moment.

But I am starting back to work any minute now, in fact, having had only a week of the two weeks I was supposed to take sick. I think, in a sense, I have always got to live like that; it's my temperament as much as anything. But physically I am very, very much better here than I am either in London or in the south of England, where I grew up. This is a good part of the country for me to be in. There is a lot of space and a lot of air, and you don't realize up here that you are living in a city; it's like a village.

I'm still not a priest. I will be glad if that comes, but if it doesn't, it won't be a blight on my life, because that would be a waste. I think it will come; whether it will come before I retire, I wonder sometimes. I have got twenty years to go yet, but the process will be slow. I don't believe that it should come at all costs. I think the Church will be richer for it when it does come, because I do believe that women can add a lot to the ministry, that we can bring a lot that is good with us, and I believe it is right. But I would hate to be bitter. I met one of the retired deaconesses, who's a wonderful lady, on Minster Yard shortly before my deaconing, and she said to me, 'You know this is what we have been working and waiting for for thirty years, and I am so pleased for all of you.' And that is what I would like to be like if I am in that position when women are made priests. I think the only way I can do that is by not going through my life now thinking 'if only'. You can make a life full of 'if onlys', and outside the Church and inside the Church I have seen a great many people end up miserable because of what they can't have. A lot of living life to the full is actually accepting one's limitations and what one can't have, as well as fulfilling one's ambitions. For me, life is incredibly rich: I have already been privileged to do far more and to be in situations that I never ever dreamed I would be able to be in. That is the positive side, and while not denying the negatives, I think it is important to acknowledge both sides.

CAPTAIN HENRY NEVILE, LORD-LIEUTENANT OF LINCOLNSHIRE

WELL, basically, the Lord-Lieutenant is the Queen's representative in a county. And as such, he has to welcome any member of the royal family to the county, and make the arrangements for anything they want to do there; not private visits, obviously, but like when the Queen came to the Cathedral for the 700-year centenary of the Angel Choir. We had a great many discussions with a great many people about what should happen, and I was responsible for producing the programme for the day.

We started by knowing that she was going to arrive at, say, eleven o'clock. We knew that the service would take an hour. Then I got together with the Dean and the police and various other people, and we decided that perhaps it would be nice after the service to go into the Deanery for coffee, which, in fact, is what we did. The city were very keen to have a walkabout, as the Queen hadn't been to Lincoln for a long time, and the county council were anxious to ask her to lunch, and she'd also agreed to open the new county police station. Through talking to a lot of people, and talking to her Private Secretary, who came down to what I might call 'walk the course' and discuss the details – how long to drive to the Cathedral, how much time to have coffee, how long for the walkabout – we gradually got to a programme, which we then submitted to the Palace for her approval.

I should think the first plans for this visit would have been jolly nearly a year ahead of the event. After the Private Secretary's been down and gone through the draft programme with you,

you then have to rearrange that and send another one. If that gets agreed, then you start what I call the tidying-up operations: menus for lunch, actual lists of who the Queen's going to meet, the order of service in the Cathedral, all that sort of thing. In the case of the present Queen, she's very interested, and she definitely saw the proposed order of service and wanted it done in a certain way. I remember there were some slight changes on that.

There are all sorts of problems. Who does she meet? Who's she introduced to before lunch? Is she going to be introduced to anybody after lunch? And then discussions with the police, and endless things about the cars, and security people saying, 'You can't do this' or 'You can't do that.'

I was feeling rather nervous; it was the first time I'd been responsible for welcoming her to the county. Actually, it was not a nice day. She came on the royal train into Lincoln, and we'd arranged a guard of honour for her to inspect, which was made up of the Lincolnshire Army Cadet Force, because there aren't enough troops in the county who could possibly have been assembled – and that in itself had to mean endless training. They were drilled on the barracks square every weekend for about three months or so before that, in order that they should be reasonably smart.

Lincoln are very proud of the fact that they have a sword that was given to the county by Richard II, and it's a tradition that they present this sword to the monarch when he or she comes to the town. This was the first thing that had to be done after she had come out of the station and before she reviewed the cadets.

That went all right, and then we all drove up to the Cathedral. We didn't drive direct to the West Door, because I always think if you go through Exchequer Gate, you get that amazing effect. And I thought that might have been a rather more impressive way of coming into the Cathedral, and also let more people see her as she approached it than just getting out by the West Door. Of course, it was unfortunate that it was pouring with rain . . . but still. So we got out of the cars on the Castle Square side of Exchequer Gate, and walked through the arch – and then you see the Cathedral quite spectacularly. Although, because of the rain, the effect was rather lost. I think there was somebody there who gave her a present or a posy.

I was rather sad that it was raining, because if it'd been a day like today,* it would obviously have been much nicer. And so when we went across into the Cathedral, I was becoming just slightly apprehensive about whether the day was going to go off all right.

They have a tradition that they keep the West Doors closed virtually until the last moment, and I think there are two reasons for this. One is the dramatic effect of looking up the aisle suddenly and seeing inside – it's really rather marvellous. Secondly, purely a practical thing, if they open the West Doors too soon, there's always a gale blowing and it blows all the candles out, all the ladies' hats off, and the flowers get upset. So they keep them shut until the last possible moment.

The Dean met the Queen at The Green, that little curved wall outside where the grass is, and led her, with myself, across to the doors, and just at the last minute these enormous doors swung open, thank God, and the trumpets blared – we'd got the trumpets from Cranwell – and you saw these terrific illuminations, all the lights up inside, and it looked wonderful really. That cheered me up a lot, and also it was obvious the Queen actually enjoyed the service and was in a good frame of mind.

Then we came across to the Deanery, and Mrs Fiennes welcomed her there and we had coffee. I suppose you can't say these situations are entirely natural, but the royal family are terribly good at putting everybody at their ease; the people they talk to may be feeling the strain a bit to some extent, until they actually get into a conversation. The Queen is amazingly good at getting people to talk. Then, after precisely a quarter of an hour, we all got into the motor cars and drove down to the north side of the Stonebow, the Queen went into the Guildhall, and she was presented with another replica sword by the Mayor.

*It was a most beautiful winter morning, with crisp blue skies, and warm, shining sun.

All the councillors were grouped around the table, and the Queen and Prince Philip took their seats by the Mayor, who made the presentation and a little speech of welcome. Then we left and did a walkabout from the Guildhall down to St Mary's, Wigford-le-Way. That was very successful. It took between fifteen and twenty minutes.

We then went up to the Assembly Rooms for lunch. There were some introductions that I had to make; various people, the chairmen of the county council and the district council, a certain number of senior deputy lieutenants, a judge or two, senior county council people, and the Queen's Champion, who happens to live in Lincolnshire. It's an ancient title: at a Coronation the Queen's or the King's Champion throws down his gauntlet on the floor, so that if anybody wants to challenge the Queen or dispute her right to be crowned, they've got to fight him. It dates, I should think, from the Plantagenets, when people were always disputing somebody's right to the Crown. Colonel John Dimmock from Scrivelsby is the Queen's Champion today, and so he was there to be introduced.

We had a very nice lunch, talked about lots of things, her dogs and her trips abroad, and Scotland, and I think she asked me how long we'd been in this part of the world, and that sort of thing. I was as relaxed as one could be in those circumstances; one's always worried about what might happen next, and one has to have one's eyes open, looking round a bit. It's just that sometimes one may be able to spot something going wrong; I mean, you don't want a photographer suddenly rushing in and taking photographs just as she's about to put a lamb chop into her mouth.

Lunch ended and we had a little speech of welcome by the Chairman of the County Council. He did that very well. We drank her health, of course, and then she was introduced to a few people on the way out, one or two catering staff and one or two secretaries who'd helped me and the County Council Chairman with the work. Then we drove off to the police station, which is about three miles out of Lincoln at Nettleham. It's a great big concrete sort of elephant house. That went all right. The Queen unveiled a plaque opening it, and toured the station, looking at various departments.

And then they went back to Sandringham by car. I waved them off, feeling . . . well, feeling rather relieved that we hadn't had any obvious mistakes. Actually, I think the only mistake was a personal mistake of mine. When the royal train first pulled in, I was caught in this rather unfortunate position when they suddenly struck up 'God Save the Queen' – I was half-in and half-out of my car. I saluted and, of course, I oughtn't to have done. I should have just climbed into my car and not paid any attention to that. As a result, we got the cars in the wrong order leaving the station: her car moved off in front of the police car that I was in, and so we had to overtake it, but after that everything went fine.

They made me High Steward of the Cathedral, and they created a Preservation Trust and made me president of that. What I had to do was set up committees to try to raise money and to supervise the spending of that money on the Cathedral. We've got an Executive Committee who do that side of it, and then I've got ten area committees, which cover the whole of Lincolnshire, who have functions and raise money for the Cathedral. It actually takes quite a bit of time. When the Dean asked me to be chairman, he said, 'We'll have only one meeting a year', and I suppose there are ten or a dozen actually! And quite a lot of behind-the-scenes work goes on.

Being Catholic, I asked my Roman Catholic Bishop of Nottingham what his feelings were before I accepted this job. If he'd said, 'I don't think you ought to do anything like that,' I would have had to have made a rather difficult decision. But he said, 'You're only dealing with the fabric, you're not dealing with anything to do with the religious side of it at all. So, if you'd like to do it, I would very much support you doing it.'

THE REVEREND JOHN NURSER, CHANCELLOR

I'D called in one early January afternoon, on my way down from Scotland, taken in the Cathedral, and gone to evensong. I don't remember much about the town, but I remember it was late-ish on a very early January afternoon, and there was the light of the solus in the choir at the end of this great Cathedral. I don't know if you're old enough to remember, but most cathedrals had what we called a tortoise stove, where little men shovelled coke into great engines. I remember these stoves were lined along the side of the nave, glowing, otherwise it would have been painfully cold.

I think the power and the mystery of the building are things that must strike anyone. They still strike me now. If you are in the building after it's shut, and there's light coming through the windows from the floodlights, and the chairs are off the floor of the nave, it is a most majestically powerful space; it's hard to imagine one more so.

And, of course, Lincoln was in the largest diocese of the Middle Ages. It was a wealthy diocese, and so the Cathedral was built on a sort of no-expense-spared basis. It was the tallest building in Europe, in the world perhaps. And I think there's a sort of hubris, both in terms of holiness and in terms of size, really. I think the building leads people to expect too much or to operate at a level that is beyond the general run of human sustenance.

It has the sort of power that only a great piece of art has. It's almost too ambitious. It's very much the creation of St Hugh, who was a Carthusian monk, and I suspect was a genuine holy man, and therefore spent more than half of his life in silence and apartness. I think that to translate that kind of holiness or that kind of closeness to God into a building in the market-place can be really quite dangerous. I think that the highest kind of spiritual activity is extremely dangerous, as illustrated by the stories from the Old Testament – of Noah staggering along with the ark, and they were just about to roll it off the cart, and somebody put out his hand to stop it and was struck dead by Jaweh, just for being too close to that which was holy.

It's a very strange building in that it is so big that it is unheatable, and Lincoln is a very cold place. It has a kind of frozen heart. So there is something very daunting and non-welcoming in it as a building, not only in terms of its size and style, but because for eight months of the year it is really unusable for any human purpose for longer than half an hour, although, interestingly, the more elderly members of our congregation, the 80-year-old ladies, are the ones who attend the most regularly throughout the winter. Perhaps they just come from a generation that isn't used to central heating. But it does mean that it is extremely difficult for any normal person to pray there, and it does mean that services are not comfortable occasions.

MICK O'CONNOR, STONEMASON

I'D worked all over the place, stately homes, English Heritage, National Trust; there's a lot of work for someone in my line, particularly now. In London you can get a lot of money working in stone now, but I decided to come here for a bit of stability. I missed being at home. I was living in bed-sits in London and not getting home until the weekend, and I've got a family, so home life is important.

I don't really know how I got into stone in the first place. I drifted into it by accident, I think. I entered into the trade in my twenties, after having done a formal art education course, and did a traineeship at York. I suppose the general cliché ideas appealed to me: that it's long-lasting work and you're dealing with quality all the time – that's the great thing, you're not knocking out a thousand of the same; they're one-offs.

I suppose primarily my brief is to keep the building safe. An area is chosen for us to work on, maybe because it's posing a danger to the public. A lot of the building overlooks the pathway, the public highway, and danger in that instance is a top priority. Also we want to save items of outstanding architectural value, so that's a priority as well. There's plenty to be going on with in those two areas: you don't have to wait until something crumbles; we've got a backlog.

I've heard the condition of the stone described as multiple micro-crises – there's a lot of problems throughout the building. Stone's a natural material and it's got a finite life. All cathedrals have problems purely because of the age factor, the fact that the stone is deteriorating. Nothing lasts forever. All building fabrics are battling against the elements, aren't they? Simple rain water, for instance, is a prime destroyer of buildings.

We build in exactly the same manner as the medieval masons. We replace the stone in a similar manner, rectifying any errors as we go, but with the decorative works, obviously we don't want to rip them out and replace them just like that. So we try to conserve what's here and use it for its original purpose, as opposed to restoration, which is replacing stonework. You wouldn't have the impudence to rip out a beautiful capital, even though it might be suffering the ravages of time; it's much more an act of humility to try to conserve that thing. I mean, a man cut it out and carved it and fixed it, and it's all been done with loving care.

I'm learning daily. We all are. Every job you go on you learn the techniques of the blokes who built it, you learn their mistakes, you learn their tricks – and there are a lot of them. For instance, I don't think these buildings were built on a grand design. I think it was a very evolutionary thing. If they suddenly found that a run of moulding is going to interfere with another idea, then they'll terminate it with a nice piece of carving, like a stop or a carved head, and that's quite a clever thing. In the Nettle Yard of the Cathedral is a moulding that obviously two men had worked on. They'd interpreted it differently and one stone actually had two different mouldings on it. I had to do two separate templates for either end, and had to what we call 'cripple' it in the middle, twist it so that the two mouldings disappeared into each other, which was quite nice.

You're very aware that it's a human building, if that's not a contradiction in terms, that it's built by lots of little men running up and down ladders. There's parts of the building where you can see the chisel marks, and that's exciting because you can relate to it. When you work in stone we have a thing called 'the beat', which is the nice steady beat of the mallet on to the chisel. The regularity and steadiness of the beat is really what it's about, and when a mason gets that, he's getting there, and you can see the quality and the evenness and naturalness of the stroke of the chisel.

Technically, I would say we can do whatever they did, but I don't think we could build anything to touch this building, because we don't have the overall view. We built Liverpool Cathedral, but it's not in the same street as this one. It's a very self-conscious attempt to copy the Gothic idea; the freedom of a building like this isn't there.

When I worked at York Minster, they had thirty to forty stone staff, including trainees, carvers and apprentices, and that was very large. Durham, I think, has two. Some cathedrals subcontract. It depends how much money a cathedral's got, how desperate the work is. Here, we've got myself, we've got Don Adams, Simon Francis, Paul Atkin, all qualified stonemasons. Then we've got two trainees, that's Brian Ansell and Mark Hooper, and we've got three apprentices, 17- and 18-year-olds serving their apprenticeships.

There's plenty waiting to be done. In the best of all possible worlds we'd have a lot more men – we could employ double the masonry staff we've got now and keep busy.

For somebody who's travelled around a lot, such as I have, and worked on a lot of grand buildings, you feel being in one place is a restriction; there's a slight feeling of time passing outside somehow. But this place is so big, and it's got so many corners and hidden delights, every day you discover something new, so there's a lot of compensation there.

I'm a great enthusiast of the job. I talk to my wife quite a lot about the job, and it's only when I see her sleeping that I stop!

JACKIE OSGODBY, CATHEDRAL SHOPS

WE have two shops. Exchequer Gate just through the arches on the right, and the one inside the Cathedral called the Consistory Court Shop. I'm manager. I have about thirty volunteers coming in at all different times, mornings, afternoons, all through the week, and I also have five permanent staff.

I do the buying for both shops in league with Susan, who is the manager of Exchequer Gate. She goes along with me to the shows and exhibitions, and we see reps together, and on any new buying we consult each other. We go to three exhibitions a year. Birmingham, which is in February, that lasts a week. We go to Harrogate in July and we go to the Cathedral and Managers Conference in November, which is a good way of looking at potential stock because the exhibitors are vetted, so there are always tasteful products, ideal for cathedrals.

We try to cater for every age, every religion and every taste; we go from balloons for the young child, to spoons and sweets for the old ladies, ties and tie pins for the gentlemen, jewellery, mugs, perfume, combs, you name it. I would think there must be at least 1,000 different items. Everybody collects – the world is now a world of collectors: thimbles, for instance; we must sell 10,000 thimbles a year at £1.25. We have two baskets on the counter and every day we fill them up. We have tea towels, trays, bookmarks, hundreds of postcards; we try to stock a little of everything, and it works. We tend to go for the personalized products, so a mug will have the Imp or the history of the Cathedral on the back, spoons have the Cathedral and the diocesan shield, plates and tea towels have various pictures of the

Cathedral, and so on. We try to keep everything in the Cathedral shop under the £5 barrier.

Everybody makes mistakes. There isn't any stock that is sticking this year, but last year I bought some nursery china, which I thought was excellent, but it didn't sell. In the past we had stocked Beatrix Potter, which always went well, and I thought, let's have a change, but that was fatal. The public weren't ready!

I find people fascinating, I love watching people. You get families who have gone to the coast for the day, and it's raining and they decide, 'Let's pop in and see Lincoln Cathedral', not really sure what they are going to see or find. When they walk into the shop, a new world opens up. They don't really expect to see a commercial outlet such as this one in a cathedral, and I think it sets them at ease. And they actually then look at the building with different eyes. They look at what we are selling, and then they go back out into the Cathedral and they say, 'Oh, it's a beautiful place.' I don't think they really looked at it before; they saw it as a big daunting building, because cathedrals scream out 'The Church', and people shy away.

Foreigners are interesting. If you are talking about children, the French are the worst. If you are talking about adults, it's the Spanish. The Spanish are rude, impatient and very loud. They don't queue – the word queue doesn't exist – they shout and scream, and they push each other to get served. The French, oh dear. French children are very badly behaved, and why I don't know, because if you go to one of their cathedrals in France, you wouldn't be allowed in making the noise they make. It amazes me. They stick their chewing-gum in all sorts of strange places. I watch what they do with their gum – and I tell them what to do with their gum.

I'm London born. I have been in Lincoln only ten years. I remember first coming into Lincoln. It was late afternoon. We had been on a tour looking at pubs – my husband wanted to buy a pub – and our last call was Lincoln. They had said to me the pub is near the Cathedral, and I thought, aim for the Cathedral. We were driving up Broadgate, and you could see the Cathedral on the top, and it was about September – lovely month, September – and it was looking its best. I looked at the Cathedral, and I had lived in London and seen St Paul's, but this was different. It seemed to me that it stood out and people respected it, where in London, St Paul's and other cathedrals and churches are taken for granted. I did, I took them for granted.

My marriage split up after a while. Before I was in the public house, I had been a buyer and manager of a gift and toy shop, so I thought, 'Let's go back to what you know.' So I came to the Cathedral shop as an assistant manageress.

I don't think I settled until about three or four years after I actually arrived. Even when I worked at the Cathedral, I felt as if I was on holiday, as if I was sort of passing through and not going to stay. But it was a good feeling. Besides, I am still here and probably will remain here too. I have no intention of moving. I have re-married now, a Lincolnshire man, and my mum has moved up here too; she has a bungalow next door.

Before I came to Lincoln, I went to church once a week, but I don't know whether I was religious then or not. I think since I have come here and worked in the Cathedral, I have become more religious. Not to the effect that I am shouting religion, but I feel in myself that I really do believe now.

I have volunteers who work for me, and some of them are sad, very sad. They home in on the Cathedral; the Cathedral is their lifeline, as it was mine when my marriage split up. And you listen to their woes and tales, and you really care. In London if people told you their troubles, you didn't really listen. You might have sympathized, but when you went home you forgot all about them. You don't here. It makes you want to help people. And we help people all the time. Strangers, visitors, tourists, lost children. They say, 'Excuse me, can you tell me where . . . is?' And you talk to people. You overhear a conversation – 'Well, I've looked everywhere. I can't find the Imp,' and you say, 'You want to know where the Imp is? I'll show you where the Imp is.' Or you show them where the toilets are.

Yesterday afternoon we had all sorts of screaming children in the shop, but nobody really loses their temper, nobody actually gets cross. Everyone just lets it ride over them. You think, 'Gosh, that child is screaming,' but it doesn't bother you. Whereas in London you'd think, 'For goodness sake, somebody stop that child.'

People say I'm a nicer person, they say I've got a different aura now. I look around and listen more, and I find I sympathize more. I think when you are in London, you don't really listen to people.

I don't like to leave home, but when you do go away, on holiday, say, when you come back driving towards Lincoln and you see the Cathedral, you know you are home. It's a marvellous feeling. Aim for the Cathedral, they said.

EDNA PARKER, FLOWER ARRANGER

ALL my life I've lived in Lincolnshire. I'm from Cleethorpes, which isn't far away. The Cathedral has always been part of my life because all the large church events centre on the Cathedral, and from childhood I've taken part in any diocesan event that has come to the Cathedral. My first really vivid memory of Lincoln Cathedral was when Dean Fry was here. I came up as a small child. I suppose I would have been, oh, about 9 or 10, so getting on for sixty years ago, which is a very long time! I saw this man with a long white beard and, according to my childish view, he was very splendidly attired in all his canonicals, and I looked at this great building, and I thought, this is God himself coming out.

I've been to many cathedrals. I suppose recognizing the splendour and the beauty of all of them, you still think your own is the best, which is rather amusing – but it is a very fine one!

I do the flowers in the main part of the Cathedral, which is the Morning Chapel, the nave and the choir, and I do all the weddings and the big services, the functions in the Chapter House and so on. I've got about eighteen ladies who help me, who are all very skilled and enthusiastic.

We raise money in various ways. First of all the Dean and Chapter give us a small donation for the whole year, £75 at the present time. That doesn't go very far, and so I write at the beginning of the year to members of the congregation, and we raise a certain amount of money through this appeal. And there is a flower box in the Cathedral where visitors, if they are impressed at all, might put something in. We make a charge, which is fixed by the Dean and Chapter, for our additional work – weddings, special services and so on. That money goes into the Flower Fund, not to us; we give all our services voluntarily. This year, for the first time, the Friends of the Cathedral have agreed to pay for the flowers at Christmas time.

All flowers can look well if one avoids certain colours, such as blue – they don't show up. White and yellow are the most splendid when you're looking down the large nave. And, of course, the arrangements have to be very large to be in any way impressive: tall stems and different shapes. That's one of the important things when you're doing the arrangements, not to have all round flowers or spiky flowers, but to have a combination of shapes. I personally, and most of the ladies agree, and the Dean certainly does, like to see natural arrangements. I don't like contrived arrangements. By that I mean the sort of thing that might be all right for flower crafts but I feel doesn't look too attractive in a church. I don't think you want that sort of thing in a cathedral, so we try to arrange them to look natural and flowing.

We use a lot of the tall garden flowers, the gladioli and the lilies and the carnations, and we use the simpler things, providing they're not blue: Canterbury bells and foxgloves, and anything that is showy, like the big white garden daisies, and a lot of the yellow flowers. One of our biggest problems is we need a lot of greenery in these arrangements, so we do pillage our gardens rather drastically.

You have to go in every day when you're on duty, because the flowers have to be watered and attended to regularly. It's not just a Sunday job, you know; the Cathedral here is open all the time. As well as all the pleasure of arranging flowers, you do have to take them down and clear away all your rubbish and sweep around the floors. It is quite strenuous because of the distances, carrying the stands and the buckets of flowers and water; and for anybody doing an arrangement at the fount, which is at the East End, you do want some good legs and feet; walking backwards and forwards, it can be quite tiring.

Mrs Bilcliffe started doing the flowers in the dim past, when people didn't do very much with them, and she's now a very skilled arranger. Of course, she does the lectern and the lower stand because she's quite a short person and she can't reach up to those high ones any longer. She's very good and very happy and rather a character. She's very independent, and we try, unsuccessfully, to cushion her by perhaps carrying a stand or something for her, but she says, 'No, if I can't carry it properly, I'm not going to do it at all!' So she's very courageous and she does do very well indeed.

We feel the flowers are of significance in that they are positioned near the altars and the shrines and the reserved sacraments, and are therefore there to help us in our worship, and are done to the glory and honour of God. But we also feel they are a welcome to the people who come, and are a talking point. Many people come to look at the architecture, but some people are attracted to the flowers, which have a very homely aspect about them. They can chatter about whether they like them – 'What did you grow this from?' and so on – and this enables a friendly atmosphere. The visitors are most appreciative, and it is interesting for them when you talk about where the flowers come from, because the people from America or Australia always want to know what a particular flower is, especially when they haven't seen it in their own country.

At the High Altar now there are lilies, carnations, gladioli and gerberas. Gerberas are a tricky flower. They have a very strong, straight stalk, with a great daisy on the top, very effective. But if you don't treat them as they should be treated, which is to put them in about two teaspoons of bleach of all things, when you've left them and you've thought how splendid they look, because they're a very dominant flower, perhaps twenty-four hours later, they've all gone, woof! like that! But if you treat them properly, they will last.

Some of the ladies have certain tricks for preserving flowers. Mrs Barbieri, the hotel manager's wife, she swears by putting them in mineral water, which she presumably buys in quantities, I don't know. Some people put aspirin in, and there are prepared things you can buy. Frankly, I give mine water and hope for the best! And they do quite well, as long as you give them plenty of it. They do drink an awful lot, even in the Cathedral, which is cold.

The visitors go poking in to see how we have done the arrangements. And when they see a lovely flower, say, these lovely lilies, they want to be quite sure they're real, and so they pinch them, and they exclaim, 'It's a live one! It's real!' And I say, 'Yes, but it won't be if you go on pinching it!' Because, of course, it bruises them. But it is so well meant and it does show their interest.

THE REVEREND DAVID RUTTER, PRECENTOR

I'M a Yorkshireman, a native of the city of York, which is only seventy miles away. I come from a musical background. There've been musicians in my family since the eighteenth century, orchestral musicians, and my great-grandfather had an organ in his house on which he gave recitals. I expect they would have liked me to be a musician pure and simple, but instead I chose to be a Church musician, and to be ordained to the priesthood upon the call of God, which I couldn't ignore.

I was appointed by Bishop Riches in 1965. It was a very happy place. It had a Chapter that worked well together under the leadership of Michael Peck, who was Dean. I hope I fitted in; I was very glad to be a member of it. I believe that the running of the place has become more efficient. When I first came here, there wasn't even a telephone in the Cathedral.

I suppose the enormous increase in the number of tourists has made a great difference. Although we're not on the same tourist route as York, where you get pushed off the pavement all the time, there has been an enormous growth in the number of visitors, and that means that we have to take care of them. We have a priest on duty as chaplain in the Cathedral all through the summer. It's a ministry to the world.

The religious changes have been many. We have tried to keep pace with liturgical development in the Church, and some of the services in the alternative services book have been adopted, but on Sundays we still have quite a good mix. We have the traditional orders of service at 8.00, 11.00, 12.15 and 3.45, and then the sung eucharist at 9.30 is one of the more modern services. I hope I would be conservative when things are worth keeping, and progressive when they need to be changed.

As the mother church of the diocese, I believe we have to take a lead in these matters, and we have the resources and the plant to put on things really well. If the Church feels that a new order of service is needed, then we can demonstrate it, and the parochial clergy and their congregations and choirs can come and see and hear it done as perfectly as we can.

I think no one can fail to be impressed by the Cathedral. For myself, I suppose it is a love relationship, because the building seems so feminine: this is Our Lady's Church, and one feels her presence all the time. I see the effect it has on the worshippers who love it as a building and find it congenial to worship here, not only because it's large and grand and lovely, but because there is an atmosphere about it to which they're sensitive, an atmosphere of prayer and devotion, a stillness, and that, I think, moves people to prayer and worship.

The Cathedral has no parish, and the people who come, come because they want to. There are a few who are tenants in our properties, and the parents and families of our singers come because of that link. And there are a few, I expect, who are disgruntled and who have fallen out with their parish priest, but not many. Others come because they are drawn by the beauty of the building, sometimes by the services, sometimes by the preaching, and many by the music.

My favourite part of the Cathedral is the place where the blessed sacrament is reserved, the Chapel of St Mary Magdalene, because the blessed sacrament is the focus of our devotion, and therefore to be there is natural. Dean Peck desired his ashes to rest in that chapel, and he was a very holy man. The Morning Chapel, where I hear confessions, is a place that is very sacred to me.

My least favourite activity is worshipping in the winter-time when we have no heat on. It's pretty cold in the Cathedral, pretty cold! The organist will tell you when he's been here a little while that the condensation on the keys actually freezes. He doesn't know that yet!

It's very tiresome, my eyesight is going. It's controlled at the moment, and with the help of strong lamps and a reading glass I can manage. I read the office of matins this morning. I have to prepare things very carefully so that I don't make mistakes. It takes longer to write letters, and there are some letters that you can't do through a secretary. Many personal and pastoral letters come to my box, and it's no use having a young girl reading out a letter that begins, 'I am about to leave my husband, what do I do next?'

There is a hackneyed phrase, that it's a challenge; but it is, it puts you on your mettle in the sense that you can't let it overcome you. It doesn't alter my feelings about God in any way. I think the challenge to our faith can come in many different ways, and that doesn't challenge mine. My faith is challenged by the state of the world, and the reluctance of so many people to do the will of God, and their open defiance of Him. That brings me to tears.

Our Lord himself was challenged all the time, and great men, like St Paul and St Peter were also challenged, and they had to be equal to it.

The basis of one's faith is personal friendship with our blessed Lord, and that begins with childhood, and progresses and is kept alive by prayer and sacrament, and that must always come first. And then one gets to know him through fellow Christians, and those friendships are very precious too.

I hope my faith is strong and that can make up for physical and other weaknesses. I should like to think I have become wiser and more tolerant. I try, and I pray hard for it. I don't think anyone is tolerant in these days, but it's a grace that one learns and it's a great advantage when you possess it.

I think my pet project – though whether I'll live to bring it into action, I don't know – is to have girls in the choir. I think it is quite wrong that girls should be excluded; there's nothing in our statutes that says the singers must be male. St Edmondsbury in Ipswich had girls in the choir, but they've abandoned it now. The American cathedrals do, and some of the Scottish ones –

St Mary's Cathedral, Edinburgh, for example. I hope people will see the reason and the nobleness of it. I would like to see it happen.

CYNTHIA SMITH, CLEANER

When I was at school I used to go up to the tower, I don't know why. My friends and me, we just used to enjoy going up to the tower to see if we could recognize where we lived, and we used to pay, I think it was 1*s*. 6*d*. It isn't open to the public now except for about six weeks in the summer months and at Easter.

I remember the first time I went inside the Cathedral was when I was in the senior school, and we came for a Christmas carol concert. And my husband as he is now, I was going out with him at the time, he read the lesson, and I remember everybody turning round to look at me. I went red! But I felt proud, you know.

My first job when I left school, I learned to be a cook, and I was assistant cook on school meals. Then I started my family and I used to clean the offices at the Cathedral. When the last cleaner, Mary, left, they asked me if I'd like the job. And, of course, I said yes. I think it was because it was the Cathedral, you know. It is an important part of Lincoln, isn't it?

Mary wasn't very well; if not, she wouldn't have left. I was only talking to her on Friday, and she said she misses working at the Cathedral.

I've been here three years in May. A lot's happened to me since I've worked here. I won a car! It was Heinz Beans, they had a lucky draw, and you had to put your name, address and telephone number on the back of a label – and I won this car. Amazing, isn't it? It's a Metro City, a red one, and red's my favourite colour. And I'm taking my test in February.

Also the *Echo*, they did an article about me being the only cleaner, and that quite pleased me. And I'm going to be in your book, so a lot has happened.

My husband's an inspector at the forge. Sometimes I bore him telling him things that people have said and what I've done, and that. He'll say, 'You're always talking about the Cathedral!' And I say, 'It's because I enjoy working there.' But he's very proud. When my photograph was in the *Lincolnshire Echo*, he sent it to my mother-in-law, who lives in Australia. And he was talking to people at his work about it.

I always have a look at the noticeboard to see what chapels are going to be used, and I make sure they're clean. And then I do bits as they come dirty, like the floors and things like that. I clean the altar brasses once a week and of course the altar rail gets cleaned every night. I just have a walk round of a morning to see what wants doing. There are no tricks in cleaning a huge building like this, just the hoover, the brasso and the dusters. That's all.

People are surprised when they learn there's only one cleaner for the Cathedral. They say, 'Crikey, how can you do all that work?' But it never bothers me. Often visitors say, 'Well, I wouldn't know where to start.' But that doesn't worry me either; I just keep plodding on.

Housework is a lot easier now. Before I got this job it seemed hard, but now it doesn't and I get through the house much quicker.

I would say I'm proud to be the cleaner of the Cathedral. Because there's only one Cathedral, isn't there, and I'm the only cleaner. So I am very proud.

THE REVEREND ANDREW STOKES, BISHOP'S PERSONAL ASSISTANT

I HAD an elder brother who committed suicide when I was nearly 14; my parents fell apart, and I think that really was the first time in my life that I actually prayed for real. I can remember going into my bedroom and praying, 'If there's anyone there, help, because I can't do this on my own.' And there's no doubt at all that I was given a great deal of strength and help, simply in being given the ability to cope with the sort of heart-break and emotional trauma in the family. I think I then faced that this was real, and that you couldn't turn away from God and pretend He wasn't there any more.

I have to say that subsequently my great times of religious development and strengthening of faith in later life have been difficult times, when you're thrown back on the fundamental relationship with God, and his power to bring good out of evil. I think probably, like any relationship you have with a person, that it is not constant. There may be, if you're fortunate, a constant deep flow in it, but your consciousness of it and its importance to you is much greater at some times than it is at others. It's like one of those moorland streams that flows along on the surface for a while and then disappears underground and then pops up again; you're not terribly conscious of it, but you know it's always there.

It's been my experience again and again, just when I think I understand this relationship and I know what it's about, then suddenly I'm at a loss. It's as if God has plans and ideas and intentions that you had not imagined, and from somewhere quite unexpected he'll say, 'Hey, come on, I want you to do this or that. I don't want your life to be like it is; I want it to be something different.' And really it's not until after the event that you're able to look back and see that actually it was meant to be that way, and you're responding to his call.

I'm just doing this job, which I hadn't imagined myself ever doing, because at Christmas the Bishop rang up and said, 'Stop doing what you're doing and come and work here.' I thought I was a parish priest and that was that. But my wife and I looked at each other and talked about it and said, 'Yes, OK,' and here I am. And that's good. God, in my experience, is objective and addresses you from outside your individual life, calls you on or offers you things, makes Himself available to you. You can be uneasy with yourself and sitting uncomfortably with your life, and not really quite sure why. Then something happens, somebody does something to you, your job disappears from under your feet, or somebody dies, or you're ill, some event happens that forces a bit of an issue, and you have an opportunity to change course. Either you accept it and take the opportunity that's given you, or you reject it and go on pretending to be what you used to be, and not what you're supposed to be now.

I think it's true that for me as a priest the different things I have ended up doing have been things that were in accordance with God's will rather than career choices of my own. And I think that that's right. I don't think a priest should set out to carve a successful career for himself. I think he should seek the will of God and just let himself be available for whatever it seems he'll be useful doing.

I think some of the most significant points are the moments of real difficulty when you're actually stopped in your tracks and driven back to a sort of primal relationship with God, where you say, 'What is all this? If You're there at all, what the hell are You up to?' You question your faith and you question Him, and you question whether you've wasted your life or you've built it on the wrong foundations altogether. Really, you're putting everything back into the ring, and then that gets unravelled and a new situation, a new relationship, a new degree of faith comes out of it. Whether it always is going to come up stronger, you never know. There aren't any guarantees. It wouldn't be faith if you knew that it was always going to come up stronger.

I would say that it's at those times when the Christian is least able to depend on his own strength and competence, because they've proved inadequate, that he has to look at what his life is for, what this suffering that he's in the midst of is about. And because he's least able at that moment to rely on his own strength, he is most open to the strength and grace of God to bring good out of the evil he is in. If I've got anything useful to say to people as a priest, it is that in the midst of whatever sorrow or tragedy or suffering they're in, that is the very place that God can reach you and give you something new. Let Him.

The Gospel is about the Cross, and this is actually the hardest thing for Christians to accept: that it's in the midst of the dereliction of the Cross that God actually gives new life and makes new life. I think if you try to dodge that, then you're always dodging the main issue in life.

Of course, you try to be constant with Him, and of course you try to rejoice in good moments and say 'hurray' and give thanks and so on, and that's right. God is the God of creation, God is good, God means life to be good. But the fact remains that life is partly good and partly bad, and either you say, 'The bad bits are all God's fault, so let's hate God for them', which is really not very constructive, or you look for some way in which God deals with evil and sorrow and tragedy. What I'm saying is I believe God does bring good out of evil. And for that the symbol of Christianity is the Cross. When we talk about the Resurrection, these aren't just little things that Christians are supposed to believe in order to get ticks upstairs; they're actually the heart of the matter. If you think they're optional extras on Christianity, then you haven't started.

I would say that I personally owe an immeasurable debt of gratitude to the Church, because I think that the capacity of the liturgy and the Gospel and the Church's teaching sustain and form and strengthen my faith, my attempts to speak to God, my

Christian life, and make it all much more possible. If it had been just an individual struggle all the time, then I personally would have gone under years since.

I suppose if you were to ask any P A what the relationship is with the chap that he works for, it's complex. I always tell people that I'm a cross between a minder and a court jester. Because the Bishop has to be out a lot, out in the diocese or in London or visiting prisons, away doing the public bit of his job, there has to be somebody here who knows everything that's going on, to handle phone calls and letters and all that sort of thing. So I keep the shop, if you like. When the phone rings during the day, it's me that picks it up, not him, by and large. And there's another part of the job. Being a bishop is a very isolated position, because all the people round you either treat you with exaggerated respect, or they are people who are trying to manipulate or get something out of you, and it's very important for a bishop to have somebody to whom he can talk and who can talk to him without any of those complications.

I was priest at Holbeach Marsh before I came here. That's forty-eight miles from Lincoln, right in the south-east of the diocese. It's an agricultural area with four churches, three villages and a hamlet, very good land, some very big farms, and quite a number of smallholdings with people working very hard on them. The churches were different in style and enthusiasm, but very genuine, and we had very direct relationships with the people. We were happy there.

I would say that the Cathedral's grown on me over the years, and now that I live here and am attached to it and am lucky enough to worship in it quite often, it's amazing how it actually gets right under your skin. It's an extraordinary building.

It doesn't matter whether you're in there at seven o'clock on a cold winter morning with two or three other people, or you're there for some huge event like an ordination, when there're thousands of people and the place is humming with life, the building still is bigger than everything that is happening in it. It's a house of God that speaks of people's faith and their

Christian life down the centuries in such proportions that it's bigger than any of the people or events that are connected with it.

THE REVEREND HUGH THEODOSIUS, PRIEST VICAR

I'M single. I'd been in my previous parish for just eleven years, which was St John the Baptist, Old Malden, in south London, and I was looking for a change. I was approaching 50, and I didn't particularly want another suburban parish. It was pure chance I came here. I might equally have landed up in Cornwall or Northumberland, or anywhere. Not having dependants, it didn't matter to me particularly where I moved to.

I'm Vicar of Billingborough, Horbling and Sempringham. Sempringham is the most interesting from a historical point of view, because that is the parish of which St Gilbert was vicar and where he founded his religious order in about 1130 – it was unique because it was for men and women. The church has a lovely Norman nave.

And then there's Billingborough, where I live. Billingborough's a rather larger village and has a thirteenth-century church. Part of Horbling must be much the same age as Sempringham; it's part Norman. Curiously, all three of them are dedicated to St Andrew, as are many of the churches round here.

I'm an honorary priest vicar. That means that I sing the priest part of the service at evensong in the Cathedral. It's the sung parts of matins and evensong; the priest does the versicles and the choir do the responses. It's a very minor thing, but you obviously need to have some musical ability to do it. It's just part of one's ministry. God has given me a voice and it's something that I can do for the worship of the Cathedral. I could do it here, but when you've got a very tiny congregation you have all said services. It's a privilege, I always feel it's a privilege. I think it would be true to say, having been brought up in that tradition, having sung in a cathedral day after day after day as a small boy, it's a spiritual uplift.

My background is that I started in the cathedral choir at Salisbury as a boy. I've always had a great interest in Church music. My father was a priest; there are generations of us. My mother's family also. This may sound odd, but Lincoln always reminds me of Salisbury. My days at Salisbury as a boy were very happy ones, and I always look to Salisbury as my spiritual home.

There's something about the smell of a cathedral. I think all places have a distinctive smell, but it just struck me that Salisbury and Lincoln were very alike, and it's been confirmed since I've been back to Salisbury.

The acoustics in the Cathedral are tremendous. The feeling one gets at the way the sound carries is very similar to Salisbury. I'm always conscious of this when I do my duties, singing the priest's part. Of course, the rebuilding of Lincoln must have been very much the same sort of time the whole of Salisbury was built, the nave and the aisles are very similar, although the unique thing about Salisbury is it's all of one period. But you don't want to hear about Salisbury, you want to hear about Lincoln!

It's very difficult for the parish priest to worship on his own; you've got to have pretty firm self-discipline. It'd be much more comfortable to sit at home and say one's offices – you haven't got anybody else, apart from God, to be account able to – but I do go and say them of a morning at Billingborough. Without trying to sound too theological or, indeed, pious, as far as I'm concerned, everything that you do during the rest of the day or the rest of the week needs to stem from what you do in church.

The same thing is happening at the Cathedral, but it's happening in a much more visible way, because people actually see services going on. Of course, something goes on here every day, but not in the same quite visible way. I mean, you're not going to get visitors coming into Billingborough church at quarter past seven in the morning or quarter past five in the evening. You're lucky to get very many visitors at all in a remote village.

I would say that I need the externals, the aids to worship, of which the chief one, as far as I'm concerned, is music. I can express myself better that way. You're worshipping God in the same way, of course, but when you're doing it with the choir and with the congregation, even if it's a very small congregation, and with the other clergy in the Cathedral, it gives you more a sense of belonging than you can have when you're saying the offices entirely on your own, just by being part of something that is so much bigger than you are.

From this side of Lincoln you can't see the Cathedral. We're much too low, we're right on the edge of the Fens. So I watch out for that moment when I can see it. I leave about 4 and evensong is 5.15. I'm always a very punctual person. As I come along by the airfield at Waddington, I look for the Cathedral, and some days you can see it and some days you can't because of the mists, and I say to myself, 'No Cathedral today.'

I don't know which is my favourite season as far as Lincoln Cathedral is concerned, because as each one comes round, I think *this* must be my favourite. You drive up there in the dark in the winter; and then you notice, as the evenings begin to draw out a bit, you come back in the dusk; and, of course, in the summer you go and return in the light. I suppose an awful lot is tied up with my memories of Salisbury. I can remember very vividly various things: what it felt like as a small boy going in; it was all rather dimly lit, you went in through the porch and made your way to the vestry. It's not the sort of thing I can describe, it's much more to do with sensations. At some times of the year, I have to say, I'm taken straight back to my Salisbury days, and I can remember what it was like in the summer, the feel of going into the cool Cathedral when it was hot outside. It's such a sort of jumble really; things come to the surface at odd times.

Another fairly vivid memory is being in the choir for the service, and the rest of the Cathedral seemed to be in total darkness, but you're in a little cocoon of light. Of course, wartime, the black-out, and I remember very particularly communion services in the early morning, when they weren't allowed to put on any lights.

I remember myself quite clearly at that age. I had a nickname, and that was Skeleton. I was so terribly thin – well, I'm still pretty thin, you can count every rib! When I'm on duty in the Cathedral and occasionally a boy in the choir makes a bad mistake or something, you feel for him, because you know what it felt like. I can remember a lot. One particular boy, the one boy I was really frightened of, the only boy as far as I can remember who was ever thrown out of the choir, he's now Michael Mates, MP. Terrible temper he had as a small boy, and he was always big and square, and I was a very timid little boy, and I didn't really start to grow until I was 16, nearly 17.

Yes, I remember all sorts of things. I remember one weekly matins, there was a gastric bug going around and the boy next to me was terribly sick, and there was evidence of this as we came out in procession, all the way down the aisle. As we lined up in the vestry for the vestry prayer, and the clergy passed through us, very much as they do at Lincoln, the Bishop of Sherborne said to one of the others 'For goodness sake, that boy must have had a lot of breakfast.' And two of us overheard him and we laughed, and we both got beaten for it by the headmaster. You do remember things like that.

COLIN WALSH, ORGANIST

THE organist job was going and it looked a very good one and a step up from where I was before, which was St Albans, and so I thought I would play my cards on that one.

We all knew the job would be going from last October, when David Flood was off to Canterbury – we organists are very cliquey, we all know one another – so that's when the mafia started, the phones started going and we all wondered who's going to get it. Lincoln is one of the more senior cathedrals and, as in any career, you have a structure of places that are more up the scale than others. I suppose at the top you've got King's College, Cambridge, and St Paul's and Canterbury, and then you've got a fairly clear pecking order right down to the very small parish churches. I'd better not say which ones those are because they won't like it very much.

I was keeping my cards pretty close to my chest, and when another organist phoned up and said, 'I'm going off to Lincoln for an interview,' my response was, 'Oh, really?' until one of my very closest friends phoned up and said, 'I'm going to Lincoln for an interview,' and I really felt then that I had to spill the beans, and I said, 'Well, shall we meet for lunch?'

Five of us came up on the same day to have a series of interviews. There was a long one with the Dean and the Precentor, and then a smaller one with the Subdean, the Chapter Clerk and a couple of other advisers. Then we had lunch, we took a choir practice, and then we all went home.

I'm sure there were one or two times when I thought, 'Oh crikey, I've blown that one now. It's back to St Albans.' But then the Dean phoned up the next morning and said, 'We are going to offer you this,' so I said, 'Oh, right, splendid.'

I was an organ scholar at St George's Chapel, Windsor, for a year, also a scholar at Christ Church, Oxford, where I read a music degree. Then I was assistant organist at Salisbury for seven years, and then the organist job at St Albans came up, and I applied for that and got it. I came here after I'd been at St Albans for three years.

Lincoln makes a lasting impression on anybody. The Cathedral is the first thing you see as you come through the countryside, these three marvellous towers sat on the hill. It is a most striking piece of architecture – some would say the finest cathedral in the land, and I wouldn't argue with that. I've been trying recently to compare it with other places, and the only other two I can think of are in France, which is a beloved country of mine. There's the Cathedral at Laon in northern France, which again sits up with many towers, and Mont St Michel, obviously on a much smaller scale, but the idea of this great city and church up on high.

I've been here a week now. I think I've taken the move reasonably in my stride. I thought when I was moving, this must be horrendous if you've got a family and children to move too, but I just called the furniture movers, they packed everything up, I went down to King's Cross, got on the 6.04 with the dog, and that was it! I have to work hard at the moment just trying to sort out the house and things, but that's actually quite fun – just do it slowly and browse round the nice shops and spend lots of money, which I'm always quite good at doing. I've sussed out all the best butchers and where to get fruit and stuff like that.

It's beautiful round the back of the Cathedral. There's some nice countryside around and, comparing it with St Albans, it's remarkably free from the sort of London influence. The pace of life, I think, is slower – I mean that in the best sense, I think the priorities of life are probably better.

I've spent quite a bit of time so far in the Cathedral, because already I'm quite attached to the instrument. When I've got an opportunity, I just go in and enjoy myself, particularly in the evening. The sound of the organ when the place is locked up at night and you've got the whole Cathedral to yourself and you're in possession of this mighty machine, it is very inspiring, there's something very special about that. As you take your hands off, there's this wonderful roll down the building. There's magic there, and it appeals to my sort of romantic sense of Church music.

It's not all that dark when the Cathedral's locked up at night because the floodlighting comes in through the windows, and there's a wonderful atmosphere, a real warmth there. I remember when I was at Windsor, there was a distance between the organ screen and how you got out of the Chapel late at night, and I used to be terrified of that. There was about six feet where I used to run like hell and get the key in the door as fast as possible to get out of the place! I don't sense anything here at all, though I do lock myself in the organ loft.

This is a very fine organ. It was built by Father Willis, who built many cathedral organs about the second half of the nineteenth century; regrettably, some of those have been restored or rebuilt . . . and ruined beyond recognition. Lincoln is one of the few that is still reasonably well preserved in its original state, which makes it one of the finest cathedral organs. It has quite a gentle sound, very fair, a wonderful accompaniment organ because it is soft and has got this wonderful sweet tone. I suppose because of the sheer space of the building, a lot of it inevitably gets lost up in the tower, which is no bad thing – I rather like a grand organ rumbling away somewhere in the distance; you've got this controlled power going on.

Where Father Willis scored so well was that he seemed to have this knack of getting over the building, realizing the acoustic potential and voicing the instrument in the most favourable way possible. This one is at a tremendous advantage because it's centrally spaced. You couldn't have a better position for an instrument. Some of it is up in the traeforium and speaks remarkably well into the building.

Salisbury has a very fine voice too, and not dissimilar from this one at all. It was the same builder about twenty years before, but I think he had mellowed by the time he got here. St Albans was a more modern organ, built in 1962 as part of the baroque revival in this country. It was very much the product of the angry Sixties, a provocative instrument in its time, but none the less quite successful as a recital instrument; less successful for accompanying because it's got some fairly harsh sounds on it.

Of course, with all the cathedral organs, we're talking about your up-market instruments, we're not talking about your *hoi polloi* village churches. Lots of them are rather old bangers, I'm afraid, but then they don't have to live up to the demands that are made of a cathedral organ. In a cathedral you've got your daily services, you've got the organist and his assistant, you've got visiting recitalists coming in; it is essential to have an organ in tip-top condition. In the villages you've probably got an old dear of 93 coming in on Sunday who can just about manage to switch the thing on, let alone play it.

I think you have to be quite religious to do this job. I suppose you could do it if you weren't, but I don't think that you would communicate in the right way or be able to make the magic that it's all about. I mean, to me, a dimly lit cathedral in the middle of February, no heating, is what the whole thing is about. Or choral evensong, with just a few in the congregation – that's when it really comes to life, rather than your big diocesan occasions.

This is a job where you have some social responsibilities, and where you're not only the leader of the choir and leader of the music within the Cathedral, but far and beyond in terms of the diocese. You're trying to inspire and enthuse visiting choirs. However humble the village church is, as the diocesan organist you do your bit to try to make them feel that they're also worth it. There's a big choirs festival happening next July, and all the little village choirs come into the Cathedral and we all sing the same pieces. We keep them quite easy, but that means a lot to them and brings them all in.

I've met some of the lay clerks informally, just because they happen to live round here. They seem a nice bunch, but I think you find in this game, by and large, they usually are. They're on your side, provided you're on their side.

I'd like to think that I could be the middle man between Philip

Marshall's regime and David Flood's regime. David was very much the new school and Philip very much the old. I don't mean that in a derogatory way at all, because I think I'm kind of part of the old school myself; I mean playing the organ quite a lot during services. The new school is more the idea that the organist always goes downstairs to conduct the choir and doesn't play the organ very much himself, and a lot of modern music in the repertoire. I would like to play the organ quite a bit myself, but go down and conduct the choir; have my new pieces in the repertoire but keep quite a lot of the old, Victorian stuff. I just love filling these buildings with great Victorian noises, I'm afraid, but a bit of vulgarity never did anybody any harm, especially in a place like this.

TIM WEETMAN, FOURTH VERGER

I CAME to Lincoln because of the job. I saw the advertisement in the *Church Times*. I'd been to Lincoln a couple of times. The first time I just popped across to see the Cathedral and listen to the choir – except the bloody choir were away, weren't they! So that was a bit of a downer. You see, me and my friends, the lads from my church choir, we catch a train to a cathedral town and the idea is to go and listen to choral evensong somewhere, to have a few beers and have a look round.

I'd seen pictures before of the Cathedral and realized it was big, but it was still quite impressive, especially when you walk through the Exchequer Gate arch, the way it sort of looms up in front of you.

Basically, I do the same job as Kate, except she's more in charge. At services I carry the Beadle Pole, and I lead in the choir, which is lower rank than leading in the canons would be. I'm a sort of ecclesiastical butler. It's a bit of theatre really: every evensong you poker somebody to the lectern to read the lessons, which means we go up to whoever's doing the lesson, bow to them and lead them to the lectern. That's all theatre. We don't have to do it – they could just about find their own way – but it's been done for hundreds and hundreds of years and it just makes it a bit more interesting, especially for the tourists.

Sometimes I don't know what possessed me to do this job: the hours are rotten, the pay's crap. It narks me a bit now and again, certainly does, but I knew that from day one, so I was quite levelled out with that. After a year, the novelty still hasn't worn off, so that's not bad, is it? And it's a nice surrounding to be in.

The majority of evenings there's choral evensong, and it's great to hear it being sung. It's carried on for x-amount of years, hopefully it's going to carry on for another x-amount of years, and just to sit there and actually see it happening, that appeals to me a lot.

It's like a fridge that place, very, very cold. Your whole body can feel the cold biting in. Your feet are really cold – you go back home at night and forget bending the toes; you're out of action there.

I think you'll always discover something new in a place like this, something you've never seen before. Amos, one of the vergers, showed me a carved part of the male anatomy that is quite interesting. It's down on the south side, on the Judgment Porch, which is a nice fancy door representing Hell on one side and Heaven on the other. If you look at the centre column on the left-hand side, there's a great big penis sticking out, which is quite amusing – I mean, you don't expect that with a church really.

It's quite spooky in the Cathedral on your own. It gives me the creeps. I'm positive I've heard footsteps behind me, and I've been on edge quite a few times, like when a couple of months ago I kept on hearing this slamming sound, and that sort of gets you unnerved. The most frightening one was when I was opening up the Cathedral one morning, and went into our little vergers' kitchen, put on the kettle, opened up the Chapter House, came back in, picked up the kettle, just boiled, looked up at the shelf, and there's a bloody pigeon there staring at me with these beady eyes. The pigeon goes 'coo', I go 'aargh' and the pigeon takes off, flying into my face on the way out. I was arse over table, trying to get my breath back; that was a good one.

Well, at the moment my social life revolves around the pub, that's about it. I just go to the pub and chat to people. I do have a tendency to sort of enjoy myself in the pub. Yes, I suppose I get drunk, although I don't like to admit it half the time. The local beer of the area is Bateman's. It's not a bad pint, fruityish, but there's very few places that seem to sell it that I know. There's three pubs I go to altogether. The one up the hill I go to, they serve Ruddles County and Webster's Yorkshire, and then down at the Jolly Brewer I drink draught Bass. At the Bull and Chain you have Younger's No. 3 on tap all the time.

The Jolly Brewer's quite good. The Victoria is even smaller than the Jolly Brewer, and it gets twice as packed, and each week they have a guest beer. The Adam and Eve's a nice quiet pub with a large garden. The Morning Star is basically an old man's pub, but it's nice to go in and have a sit down. There's a dartboard but no music; nice and peaceful. There's quite a few pubs for the size of the place. It surprises me how half of them stay open.

GREG WRIGHT, LAY CLERK

WELL, this is a bit personal, really. There are several reasons, aren't there, always? All right, the most straightfoward reason I came to Lincoln was to visit a lay clerk who had been a friend of some years' standing. It was to be a thirty-six-hour visit, but, as it happened, there was an alto lay clerkship going, and he said, half jokingly, 'Why don't you go for an audition?' So I did. Within a few hours I'd had an audition and been offered a place in the choir, and pretty well decided to come. That was autumn. It hadn't started to get so bitterly cold as it does a bit later on, but I do remember the extraordinary windiness of this area just in front of the Cathedral. The wind seems to whistle along the side and whips round the corner, and I remember the violence of the wind then.

Now the background to that was a bit more complicated, and, as I said, really rather personal in a way. I had stopped teaching several years ago and had some vague notion about starting a business. I fancied being my own boss rather than someone else's employee, but I never really had commitment to the scheme, so nothing much came of it. I was drifting about not doing very much, and this was an opportunity of doing something different and something rather more definite than I was doing. That was part of the reason. The other was that last year I suffered a broken relationship, and I actually felt that I needed to go away from where I was living, and that was quite the most important factor really.

The relationship was something of a first for me. I lack experience in affairs of the heart, and at the age of 39 a first of that sort is certainly a very traumatic experience. It's difficult to say why it ended or why it has been so painful. It was painful because it was the first time, I guess. It was painful because I didn't expect it to finish, and it was painful because I was vulnerable for all sorts of psychological reasons.

So I've escaped, I've escaped into a sort of limbo and that's why I'm here. In one sense I don't know why I'm here and I don't know what I'm doing, and I don't know what I shall be doing next year. I knew that I was going to have a sense of isolation. I had some very close friends of long standing down in Kent, and those friends were very important to me. I knew that I would feel that I had been torn away from there.

I must confess I've been disappointed at the extent to which established people here have not gone out of their way to be hospitable, to make me welcome. They haven't been unfriendly by any means, but they haven't actually gone out of their way to make me feel at home, and I think they needed to have done really if I weren't to have gone on feeling this sense of isolation.

Fortunately, there is a sort of ready-made social group at the house, because there's a group of us who are Cathedral employees, mostly lay clerks, living at 27 Minster Yard. It has something of a studenty atmosphere about it, a sense of community, which is very appealing. That's a great plus point, and without that I don't think I would have coped at all; I think I would have gone shooting back to Kent after a month or so.

Although many of the reasons for coming here were overwhelmingly negative, nevertheless the opportunity of singing in a cathedral choir in such a magnificent place as this was extremely appealing in itself, and, indeed, in many respects it has been rewarding. I find the building and the environment endlessly inspiring. It still shocks me to come out of 27 Minster Yard and to see that edifice, especially late at night when the building is floodlit, and I simply stand and stare at it, looking up at the great Central Tower, almost as it were, in amazement. I suppose I must look rather like a tourist seeing it for the first time. The sheer scale of the thing fascinates and overawes, and the beauty of the decoration, the wonderful stone carving under the organ on the screen, that always fascinates me.

I think I was aware when I came here that living on the doorstep of a place of worship as inspiring as this would make it easier for me to develop a spiritual life, and there have been occasions when that's proved true. The fact that one is passing through it daily, and that there is an opportunity to go into the Morning Chapel, for instance, which has been a place of prayer for many, many hundreds of years, that circumstance is likely to inspire one to feel more spiritual. But the spiritual life is not something, I believe, that grows consistently through life; it's something that sometimes is very strong and sometimes not. Mostly there are periods of aridity and disappointment, which are broken by occasional insights and periods of revelation, or increased wisdom, or whatever.

For someone like myself, who hasn't had much experience, it's hard singing in the choir. The sight-reading is demanding. You have to sing a lot of right notes with very little preparation, sometimes no preparation at all. It makes demands on the technique. Modern music in particular tends to demand a very wide *tessitura*, particularly for altos. I've had some considerable difficulty with upper notes; I'm much happier on the lower alto range.

Choirs are divided into two distinct groups: cantoris, which is the choir on the north side of the cathedral, and decani, which is the choir on the south side of the cathedral. It is quite an important feature of cathedral music and cathedral choirs that in antiphonal settings one can hear the music moving from one side to the other, and the same in psalm singing, where one verse will be sung by can. and the next by dec., and so on. There is quite an amusing sense of competition between the sides, and if you happen to have a certain group of characters on one side there's quite likely to be a musical difference. The boys on one side, for instance, may have a more muscular tone, or one side might be better at ensemble attack than the other. I must confess there is a little bitchery, complaining about the weaknesses of technique or sight-reading of the guys on the other side.

Recently I've been spending rather more time in the Cathedral during the day, doing my second job. My second job hasn't got a formal title because it's a rather haphazard arrangement, like so many things here. I suppose I would call myself the organizer of the reception team. The reception team is a group of round about a dozen people who stand at the West End of the Cathedral in order to welcome tourists, and encourage them to part with some money. I organize that team and the rotas, and I deal with the money that's collected, bank it and so on. It's not a very demanding job, there's nothing creative about it, and one would hope that something a little more exciting will come up eventually. But it is a terribly important second job, because it provides an important income.

The established members of the team are rather good at eliciting money. It is meant to be a contribution, not a charge, certainly not a charge. In fact, a year or so ago there was a till and people were actually paying a sum to go into the Cathedral. That was very unpopular with the people who had to operate it, never mind the tourists themselves. But now it's done rather more gently than that. If a tourist looks to be unwilling to part with his money, the most you could say is something to the effect, 'If you would like to make a contribution, put it in this chest here.' You mustn't say anything stronger than that; it just wouldn't be the right thing to do. But it works, and the people who are a bit reluctant part with their cash.

Members of the team often comment on how devious people are if they decide that they don't really want to part with their money. They actually have it ready in their hands, but kind of sidle past hoping to get away without being spotted by members of the team, even though, of course, every tourist has a perfect right not to donate anything. If you've nabbed them by saying, 'If you'd like to contribute, sir . . .,' then they'll go and do it, even if they don't want to. It's very curious.

I'm sorry to say that there is a particular nationality that is known by everyone to be apparently mean as far as donations are concerned – the Germans. I think part of the reason is that in Germany the churches are subsidized by the state. In fact, there is a tax, I believe, which helps to support church buildings, and that could be the reason. At any rate, very often Germans just don't seem to be willing to part with the cash.

There are quite a lot of Italian visitors, and they're a bit reluctant as well. They give me the impression that they expect to be cheated and are therefore no more generous than they have to be.

Middle-class English people, I suppose, are the most reliable in the sense that they tend to donate what is suggested. There is a noticeboard in the Cathedral: '£1 per person or 20p for a child or OAP is the suggested donation', and they will tend to donate that sort of sum.

It's only in the last few days that I've begun to feel that maybe there could be a future for me in Lincoln, and that I might actually belong here one day. I don't know why. Perhaps that's influenced by the fact that it happens to be summer and there's a bit of sunshine. It may pass when the wind starts whistling round and it's absolutely freezing cold in the winter, and if I still haven't met anyone, I shall feel just as wretched as ever. But having spent the first half of my adult life as an apparently contented bachelor, I now believe that I'm not really ever going to be contented unpartnered, and that will have a far greater effect upon my happiness than anything else.

I was very doubtful whether or not the subject of my being gay ought to be mentioned, because one does feel vulnerable. At the same time, I have a strong instinct to be honest and I think it's an extremely important facet of what and who I am, so it would have been unsatisfactory in some ways not to have mentioned it.

My social life so far has been rather limited to outings to the pub with the lads at 27. I make efforts to join other musical groups and so on, but it seems to take time for that kind of thing to develop. I've tried to involve myself in voluntary work: I do a little adult literacy teaching, I've just recently become involved in the talking newspaper for the blind for the Lincoln area, and I also decided that I might like to become a Samaritan. It's building up; things are starting to look a bit brighter.

The gay social life in a town like this depends terribly much upon either the existence of an established gay pub or upon the efficiency of a formal gay group. The gay group in Lincoln is not very efficient, so that the venue that it creates, which is a fortnightly amateurish little disco in an upper room of a pub, is no great thing, although recently they have also put on a social evening once fortnightly, which is a very low-key, fairly sociable sort of thing; well, that's something.

I'd like to be open about being gay, but I don't think that in Thatcherite Britain in the Eighties one can feel terribly happy about being completely open. And, unfortunately, I don't think one can feel completely happy about being open in the Church at the moment. However, having said that, there are a number of people here who are – how shall I say? – like-minded, and I think the younger generation are far more open and relaxed about sexual orientation than the older generation. The guys at 27 are quite relaxed about it one way or the other, and that's wonderful, because it means that one can simply be oneself there, and that's important.

SELECTIVE GLOSSARY

ARCHDEACON — A bishop's administrative officer; also engaged in the practical, legal and pastoral work in his part of the diocese.

BISHOP — The chief minister in an episcopally ordered church, who is usually in charge of a diocese.

CADAVER TOMB — A tomb exhibiting a sculpture of a skeleton.

CANON — A clergyman on the staff of a cathedral or collegiate church, or a title of honour within a diocese.

CATHEDRA — The bishop's throne in a cathedral; usually near the altar and eastward of the choir stalls.

CHANCEL — Eastern part of a church (often called the Sanctuary); usually the area containing the choir and the altar. Also a screen of lattice work by which a chancel was separated from the nave, mainly in medieval times.

CHANCELLOR — One of the dignitaries in an Old Foundation (q.v.) cathedral. He is concerned with the cathedral school and library.

CHANTRY — A medieval chapel originally endowed for the saying of Mass for the soul of the founder.

CHAPTER — A corporate title for the dean and canons of a cathedral, who are responsible for all aspects of the life of the cathedral.

CHAPTER HOUSE — The place where the chapter meets for business.

CHOIR — The part of a church used for an organized body of singers, also applied to those who sing there.

CLOISTER — Covered arcaded walkway around an enclosed area, which is usually lawned.

DEACON — The lowest order of the Christian ministry, below the bishop and priest. The term is applicable to both men and women who may undertake the tasks assigned to priests except to preside at Holy Communion and hear confessions.

DEAN — Head of a chapter in a collegiate or cathedral church. A cathedral dean is also the senior priest of the diocese.

FAN VAULT — Almost flat, cone-like vaulting. The ribs and panels resemble a fan with a heavy, elaborately carved keystone.

FOUNDATION — Pertaining to the establishment of cathedrals. About half of the medieval cathedrals were monastic and half were secular. With the dissolution of the monasteries during the Reformation, the monks in cathedrals were replaced by secular clergy and were given a new constitution by Henry VIII; those cathedrals are known as cathedrals of the New Foundation. Cathedrals that always had secular clergy, of which Lincoln is one, retained their old constitutions and are known as cathedrals of the Old Foundation.

MAGNA CARTA — The great Charter, the basis of the English Constitution, obtained from King John in 1215. Many exemplars were issued (probably thirty-six). Only four are known to still exist: one is in Lincoln Cathedral, one is at Salisbury and two are in the British Library in London.

PRECENTOR — A priest responsible for the choral services.

PRIEST — An ordained member of the clergy empowered to celebrate the Eucharist and to pronounce absolution of sins. Second in line of ordained seniority: bishop, priest, deacon.

PRIEST VICAR — Priest who leads the singing during worship, normally with cathedral choir.

RETROCHOIR — The part of a cathedral church behind the high altar.

RITE A — An order of service for Holy Communion for the Church of England in modern language, in the Alternative Service Book.

RITE B — An order of service for Holy Communion for the Church of England in the more traditional language, in the Alternative Service Book.

VERGER — A lay official who carries a symbol of office before church dignitaries; also one who is responsible for cleanliness and good order in the church.